"Ryan is extremely knowledgeable, helpful, and easy to work with. He won't lead you astray and will do everything he can to make sure you get the best deal possible." – Matt and Kristy K.

"Ryan Hoffman is, in my opinion, the most honest and genuine real estate agent in the area. I would recommend no one other than Ryan Hoffman to any of my friends or relatives looking to buy or sell a home" - Doug and Audrey C.

"Ryan did a great job helping us sell our home. He did exactly what he said he would do from awesome photos, to Facebook Ads. We had a contract in about 2 weeks after he told us he was advertising it online. He was very easy to work with, laid back and definitely a smart guy! I would definitely recommend him if you want a stress free easy sale!" – Erin M.

"Ryan's honest, practical approach to the real estate process was unmatched! He helped us to negotiate a fair price for our dream home, was immediately responsive to questions, and easily managed a transaction with several moving parts. Ryan was ever present in our lives for several months, so much that our children looked forward to his visits! We will forever be appreciative of all of the hard work he put in to making our lives better. Thanks Ryan!" – Bob and Laney L.

"After two years of no luck in selling, Ryan got it done within 16 days with hands on service and responsiveness, great pictures and video, and a strong social media presence. Thanks again Ry for all the help. I would recommend Ryan to any seller or buyer looking for a new, fresh approach to the real estate game!!" - Jared and Ivona H.

"I had a home in Albany that I tried to sell twice, both times through very big and well known realty companies What blew me away was that Ryan did more work to sell my home than both of the previous "traditional" agents combined. He took calls, forwarded information, advised me on the market and on offers, put up signs, printed flyers, made a tour video... I was amazed at all the work he did. I can say with 100% certainly that my house would not have sold without his help" – Andy C.

"Ryan did a very professional job for us. He is a no B. S. honest person. He helped us get though the process for contract to closing. We had 2 offers from him after having none is 2 years with another company." – Jim and Carol R.

"He is an excellent agent. He is very honest and worked really hard to get me the best deal on my house. He was really easy to communicate with and was available to show me the house many times. I highly recommend him." – AJ M.

"We then enlisted Ryan as a sellers agent, and his services were exemplary. He worked very hard for us, was always available, returned calls quickly, and has excellent knowledge regarding all phases of the process. He lined up qualified, serious buyers to look at our house, and we sold it very quickly with minimal disruption. I would highly recommend him to anyone buying or selling a home" - Carl C.

DEFEND YOUR EQUITY

PRICING YOUR HOME IN THE CAPITAL REGION FOR MAXIMUM PROFIT

Ryan Hoffman

DEFEND YOUR EQUITY: Pricing Your Home in the Capital Region for Maximum Profit.

© 2017 Ryan Hoffman

All rights reserved. No portion of this book may be reproduced, stored in a retrieval system, or transmitted in any form or by any means – electronic, mechanical, photocopy, recording, scanning or other – except for brief quotations in critical reviews or articles, without prior written permission of the publisher.

Published by: Leverage Real Estate LLC
Printed in the United States of America

ISBN-13: 978-1976386282
ISBN-10: 1976386284

Limit of liability / Disclaimer of Warranty: While the publisher and author have used their best efforts in preparing this book, they make no representations or warranties regarding the accuracy or completeness of the contents of this book. The publisher and author specially disclaim any implied warranties or merchantability of fitness from a particular purpose, and make no guarantees whatsoever that you will achieve any particular result. Any case studies that are presented herein do not necessarily represent what you should expect to achieve, since selling your home depends on a variety of factors. We believe all case studies and results represented herein are true and accurate, but we have not audited the results. The advice and strategies contained in this book may not even be suitable for your situation, and you should consult your own advisor as appropriate. The publisher and author shall not be held liable for any loss of profit or any other commercial or personal damages, including, but not limited to, special, incidental, consequential, or other damages. The fact that an organization or website is referred to in this work is a citation and/or potential source of information does not mean that the publisher or author endorses the information of the organization or website may provide or the recommendations it may make.

This publication is designed to provide accurate and authoritative information in regard to the subject matter covered. It is sold with the understanding that the publisher is not engaged in rendering legal, accounting, or other professional services. If legal advice or other expert assistance is required, the services of a competent professional should be sought.

AKNOWLEDGEMENTS

To my parents, Cindy and Joe who have encouraged me throughout my life and my career, to always keep trying and to remain patient in route to achieve my goals. Thank you for your countless efforts to promote my services and help me in ways that go beyond just a simple referral. Thank you for being the parents that most people would envy.

To my sisters, Sarah and Lauren, who have always supported my efforts and are my self-proclaimed #1 fans. (Tied for 1st) They have always tried their best to encourage me, listen to ideas, and have become evangelists of my many messages, themes, and beliefs. Thank you for all your help and efforts you have shown me over the many years.

To my wife, Erin, who deserves much credit for riding the roller coaster with me, and has been my confidant, and business consultant. Thank you for taking the time to listen, endlessly, to my many ideas, struggles, joys and frustrations that the real estate industry had shown us, and my desire for entrepreneurial freedom in this life. You have shown exquisite patience and belief in my potential and abilities. You have kept me motivated, picked me up while I was down, and helped me overcome many struggles in business and in life. Without your encouragement, I may not have believed in myself enough to make this book and many other things, a reality. I will never forget what you have done, and continue to do for me on a daily basis.

To my friends and other family members who have done their best to also encourage others to speak with me in an effort to achieve their real estate goals, and for continually inquiring on my progress and wishing me the best in life and business.

To my many past clients, I am grateful and thankful, that you had the confidence to work with me, and entrust that I could help you overcome your real estate obstacles and challenges. I am flattered that you have chosen to work with me, in an industry that offers you many other choices. I hope I have left you feeling confident in the outcomes we have achieved together.

Disclosure: In order to abide by real estate rules and regulations, some of the local home sales referenced in this book will remain private and the physical address will not be shared. This is the case for home sales that were represented by other real estate agents in the region. If you're interested in learning more about the details of these particular home sales described in this book, reach out to me and I will share these comparable sales with you.

TABLE OF CONTENTS

Introduction | **1**

Real Estate Statistics | **7**

Key Factor #1 | **21**
Location

Key Factor #2 | **35**
School District

Key Factor #3 | **51**
Taxes

Key Factor #4 | **61**
Condition

Key Factor #5 | **87**
Timing

Case Study #1 | **101**
239 Beaver Dam Rd.

Case Study #2 | **113**
53 Rooney Ave.

Case Study #3 | **125**
16 Drummer Dr.

Case Study #4 | **141**
9 Mason St.

Case Study #5 | **153**
15 Wolfert Ave.

What's Your Home Worth? | **167**

About the Author | **169**

INTRODUCTION
Real Estate is driven by Supply and Demand

by Ryan Hoffman

In 2015, tragedy struck a small town here in Upstate New York that most of us probably figure would never happen around here, something we only see on the news, across other parts of the country. But the reality was, it did happen here and it's something that could become even more prevalent in this country in the very near future. It was a water crisis.

Hoosick Falls, while not a hub of the Capital Region, is still situated in one of the four main counties (Rensselaer) and is at least in driving distance to the City of Albany and other popular amenities that one may find convenient and alluring.

In the Fall of 2015, news reports first popped up about a possible contamination in the public water system and to no surprise, caused widespread panic and concerns throughout the small village. It was even picked up on the national news stage. A situation like this takes precedence over anyone's real estate goals, although the homeowners largest investment of their lives is surely affected, their health concerns were and will remain, much more important.

But as menial as it may seem compared to selling a home, this water crisis had, and continues to have, a big impact on the Hoosick Falls real estate market. For those who wish to sell their home in Hoosick Falls, the contaminated water crisis is sure to be on everyone's radar. It is stressful enough selling a home, let alone trying to sell a home in a town where the entire population, and even the entire Capital Region, is aware of a water crisis that could be a serious risk to one's health.

In 2015, the final average sale price for all homes within the Hoosick Falls, NY Zip Code of 12090 was $121,734. By the end of 2016, just over 13 months after the water crisis was first reported, the average sale price fell to $85,367. Coincidence? I don't believe so.

To further this point, just so you know how the statistics had played out, the total number of homes that sold in 2015 which averaged the $121,734, was a total of 46 homes. In 2016, the number of homes sold in the entire year was 39, averaging, again, $85,367. Only a difference of seven home sales, but an average loss of over $35,000 in equity.

Hoosick Falls, NY 12090 Zip Code Real Estate Stats*

2015: 46 Homes Sold. Average Sale Price = $121,734

2016: 39 Homes Sold. Average Sale Price = $85,367

Courtesy of the Eastern NY Regional Multiple Listing Service from 1/1/2015 to 12/31/2016.

Throughout this book I will continually prove how real estate, and the sale of homes in the Capital Region, is driven by Supply and Demand. While you may already know this as common knowledge, it seems to have been lost within an industry that is dominated by hundreds of thousands of licensed real estate agents who lead consumers to believe that they hold the secret responsible for the sale of your home.

This isn't just a localized epidemic, this is the state of the real estate industry across the globe. A low-barrier of entry and the handcuff business model, allows agents to gain a foothold on your equity and attempt to care about your bottom line, all while holding you hostage until another agent comes forward with a buyer.

Not every agent is this way, but research, surveys and polling, combined with my own personal experience, have all led to the same conclusion from the general public in regards to the integrity of real estate agents, and the results are far from positive.

Point being, the sale of your home is not determined by the agent you choose, unless of course they believe in the key factors that are laid out in this book. As a practitioner working on the inside, I see the redundant marketing messages that have been spewed onto the general public for almost half a century.

What has been lost among all the noise of the 3,000+ agents and 400+ registered brokerage firms in our area, is the fact that houses, ultimately sell themselves. Some real estate agents are no stranger to this reality which is why they rely on gimmicks and other marketing tactics to alter your perception in an effort to win your business.

A good example of this would be the use of the long-term agreements agents use to submit your home onto the Multiple Listing Service (MLS). Most agents don't know when your home will sell or how to even arrive at an accurate price point for your home, so they tend to simply overprice it from the onset and wear you down with price reductions over the course of six to twelve months.

You may judge for yourself, but the cause of this rant is rooted in just one ideology. That is, when you understand the marketplace and the key factors that lead to the sale of your home, you will see that **your home sale is market driven**, and your home buyer is already out there looking for a home just like yours.

When referring to Hoosick Falls, and the disappointing reality of a water crisis, one look at the year-on-year statistics for home sales should be enough to put things into perspective. Granted, Hoosick Falls may not be the example you were expecting when it comes to defending your equity and pricing your home correctly for the highest profit possible. But it is an important starting point that uncovers many truths about selling a home that you will discover in this book.

If a real estate agent is responsible for the sale of your home, as they love to take credit for, then have all the agents that work in Hoosick Falls suddenly become incompetent? If agents love to market their recent "sales", saying they were solely responsible, then where are they when things don't quite go their way?

Market conditions rule the sale of your home, not the agent who you have chosen to put their sign in your front yard.

In 2004, homes were selling with ease. Over 90% of all homes listed on the market sold easily in many areas of our region. Of course we all know what happened next, by 2007, the "housing crisis" and "financial collapse" sent panic waves throughout the country. Once the crisis hit, home prices plummeted, and homes languished on the market for months on end. Had real estate agents suddenly become zombies?

This is obviously an absurd gesture, and I see many real estate agents perpetuate a recent home sale as their own doing, all in an effort to win more business. It's common sense to use this tactic and social proof is definitely alive and well in growing a business. But if agents are so quick to take responsibility for the sale of your home, where are they when the home fails to sell?

The common strategy that exists today for pricing a home is to take the three most recent sales in your area, divide by three and wa-la, your price is set. Well, heck, you can do that. In the age of Zillow and other online instant-home valuation sites, you don't need an agent to take some sale prices and divide by three.

But the truth is, there usually is no pricing strategy among most agents to position your home to sell in defense of your equity. It's nothing more than a numbers game for them. "Everyone has one sale in them" is the common motto throughout the industry. And if brokers hire 100 agents, and each agent sells one home, then the brokerage firm can take credit for 100 home sales. This is the false reality that homeowners fall into time and time again. My point is, agents are not trained in pricing a home to make you the most money, they are trained in winning the most business and getting you locked into a long term agreement.

They use their office of agents to create a false reality of success by way of power in numbers. When you list your home with the typical agent, you can forget about getting the best price. Agents need turnover, agents just want as many listings as possible.

Agents only make money if your home sells, and they need it to sell as quickly as it hits the market. They have no time to try and get you the best price, because this is not what agents are trained to do. Agents are trained to win your business through gimmicks, and brain-wash advertising, which creates a perception that some consumers often mistake as reality.

The reason I am writing this book is because, I am a Realtor, but I am a Realtor by default. I don't fit in. I don't have a sales script or a gimmick to use. I don't follow the industry standards of being an annoying pest, begging for business. I also see homeowners being undersold. Specifically, homeowners who have a lot of equity, and live in high demand areas where homes are selling very quickly and easily.

What I am about to reveal to you will drastically change your outlook on the sale of your home. You will no longer be worried about which agent or firm to choose, instead, you will only be worried about the current market your home is located in, and how you can position it for the highest profit possible by using the key factors laid out in this book.

I will explain to you how pricing a home should be done, with real world examples using real home sales right here in the Capital Region. Homes which may just be located in your neighborhood. You will see examples, of all the 5 Key Factors at play, using 5 case studies from home sales which resulted in the owners selling the home for the best possible price by using the 5 Key Factors to price the home correctly.

But first, I need to start with a quick introduction on my statistical model, focusing on the real estate data that we should care about the most. No worries, this next section will be quick and painless.

It will allow you to follow along, throughout this book, with a clear understanding of how we are weighing the local real estate data to sell a home for the best price and what it means for the sale of your own home.

I assure you at the end of this book, you will be more confident, and more aware of what your home is worth, and how easily it can really be to sell your home once you line up the **5 Key Factors** and **Defend Your Equity**!

REAL ESTATE STATISTICS
Understanding the context of the stats we discuss

by Ryan Hoffman

Throughout this book, when speaking of all real estate statistical data, it is important that I point out the criteria that goes into all this statistical information. Let me give you an example in an effort to clarify this easier.

Let's say I post the following basic numbers about all the home sale data in a particular zip code. For this example, let's pretend this is the basic sales data for zip code 12110 in Latham, NY for the entire 2016 calendar year: (Not actual data just a hypothetical example)

Figure 1.1: Real Estate Stats for 12110 zip code. All of 2016

Homes Listed	Homes Sold	Average Sale Price
350	250	$250,000

Now, it is important to realize that when I run statistical analysis and research it follows a strict criteria. When I state that 350 homes were listed for sale, what do I mean by that? Every and any home in this particular zip code? The answer is no, and here is why. The overwhelming majority of home sales consist of Single-Family home types. But if I were to count all other home types, the statistics would not be accurate, nor would be helpful for you to use and measure against your own home sale.

When doing the statistical research of the overall housing market, other home types can be included in this search. The additional home types consist of Two-Family homes (including Duplexes), Commercial properties, Vacant Land and New-Construction homes. Except I never include these property types in my analysis.

If you own a 3-bedroom Ranch home in Latham, then looking at overall sales data and averages that include Two-Family homes, Commercial property, land, rentals and other types, would skew the overall averages, and thus, give you the incorrect value of your immediate market.

Again, let's say you own that 3-bedroom Ranch style home in Latham, and it was built in 1965. Do you think your home's value is comparable to homes that were built in the past year or two? Obviously, expecting your 1965 Ranch home to sell for the same price as a 2017 Ranch home, even if the floorplan, lot size, and every other detail were exactly the same as your home, is unrealistic and probably common sense that I need not explain to you. But take solace in the fact that, throughout this book, when I speak of housing data, all data I discuss does not include the criteria mentioned above but rather **only includes Single Family home types**.

Another side note worth mentioning is that Single-Family home data **does** include Condos and Townhomes. While they are considered "Single-Family Attached" (shared walls), compared to the common, Single-Family Detached home, it still is important to know that Condos and Townhomes are included in the overall averages.

Now, of course, I know that a 3-bedroom Townhome has zero in-common with a 3-bedroom Ranch home, which is why some of the examples you will see throughout this book include segmenting the overall data down to various types of home styles, features and sizes (bedrooms, bathrooms, square footage). You will see throughout this book that looking at overall averages is never enough. We must always go in-depth, well beyond the starting point of simple housing market data.

To Recap:

1. New Construction home sale data, Two-Family home sales, Commercial Properties, Vacant Land and Rentals, are not included in any of the statistical totals and averages discussed in this book. They are never considered or used, nor should be used, when pricing a Single-Family home for sale.

2. Townhomes and Condominiums, are included in the overall statistical totals and averages in this book. However, segmenting the data, as it pertains to each individual type of home style, is important and is always a part of analyzing and pricing a Single-Family home for sale.

3. When segmenting the real estate data to research home values, I always start with the zip code and the school district, and then I drill down from there. The process looks something like this: Zip Code > School District > Home Style > # of Bedrooms > and so on.

It is required that I note that all statistics are courtesy of the Eastern NY Regional Multiple Listing Service (ENYRMLS) for the timeframes between 1/1/1996 and 12/31/2017. This is the official Multiple Listing Service (MLS) of the Capital Region, covering eight counties in our area. This is the same Multiple Listing Service that local agents, including myself, are a member of and use as the main platform to market a home for sale. (Even though there are other options to sell your home) Thus, this source, and its data, is vitally important when it comes time to sell your home. Regardless of the direction you choose to go in when you sell, you can, at the very least, understand what I call the 5 Key Factors for pricing your home, which can and should result in higher home sale profits for you.

Statistical Categories

In this book, and when pricing your home, there are nine statistical categories that I look to every time I research and price a home for sale. The great thing about statistics is that they are irrefutable. This is why I disclosed which criteria I use when I pull a list of local home sales. (Single-Family homes only)

If Ranch homes are selling for $250,000 in Latham, then listing yours for $300,000 is sure to waste up to a year of your life, and ruin your overall price in the end. Of course data and analysis is most likely mundane information to you and enough to make your eyes glaze over. That may be true, and understandable if so, but if you're reading this book you have at least some interest in learning how selling your home for the most money can happen.

If 100 homes are listed in a particular area, where by the end of the year, 50 of those 100 have sold, we would see 50% of inventory selling. This isn't bad, but not great either. But wouldn't you like to know how many homes have sold in your zip code, or even in your neighborhood, when compared to the amount of homes offered for sale? You should. The answer to this question, or better said, discovering the statistical performance of your area and homes like yours, is the first initial step into uncovering a slew of information that can tell you exactly how your home sale will fare within the marketplace. Sure, there are many different categories, each meaning different things, (good or bad) but once combined, this information can be used as an overall guide to predicting the performance of your home sale in the local market.

Here are the nine categories that I will reference throughout this book.. Getting an idea of what these categories are and how they can measure a home's value, is critical towards following along and understanding how you can unlock the ultimate value of your home.

1. <u>Total Homes Listed</u>

The number of homes to be offered for sale on the MLS in a county, zip code, or even a neighborhood, provides direct insight to the amount of housing volume an area is putting on the market. The number of homes listed fluctuates month to month, and year to year. **This is the Supply when it comes to Supply and Demand**. How many homes are available? Was there this many homes for sale last year at this time? Seeing a drop in Supply, while Demand remains steady, or increases, means an increase in your sale price. Think about this in the retail market space for example. If Apple Inc. decides to produce just 500 iPhones this year, what do you think will happen to the price of the phone with so many people using iPhones? The sale price will skyrocket with low Supply and high Demand.

2. Total Homes Sold

This is the Demand indicator of the housing market. If 100 homes are listed for sale in 12 months, and all 100 sell, it's safe to say Demand is pretty high. **And when Demand is high, so is your sale price.** There are nuances to this, of course. Some areas of the region list only 35 homes in a single year. Others list 700 homes or more in a year. But regardless of the supply, the amount of homes that sell in reference to the overall supply is still telling the same story. If the town of Berne only lists 35 homes a year, but all 35 homes sell, that is proof that a small little market on the outskirts of Albany County has demand regardless of the low volume.

3. Percentage (%) of homes sold

If 100 homes are listed on the market, and 50 of those sell, that means sellers have a 50% chance of success. Some markets in our area, as you will see, have selling ratios upwards of a 90% success rate, and you probably won't be surprised when you realize what areas those are. The percentage of homes sold is simply a shortcut for your eyes. When you see that percentage total, you can quickly determine how "hot" a market is. Ratios above 60% usually means high demand, or demand is steady but supply is down.

4. Average Sale Price

Obviously, average sale prices are a big factor and the most common statistic or question on the minds of home owners everywhere. The average sale price is important, of course, and carries even more weight when viewed on a deeper scale. For example, if I told you that the average sale price in Clifton Park (12065 zip code) was $278,000, what could you really do with that information? Well maybe it's a good starting point, but it's only an overall average for the entire 12065 zip code. If you went deeper, you would see that the average sale price changes when you segment the home sales based on style, size and other amenities.

For example, what would you think when you learned that the average sale price for a **Colonial style home** in Clifton Park was $325,000 while the average sale price of a **Ranch style home** was $265,000? This is a big difference. If you just looked at the overall average sale price of the zip code ($278,000), and you own a Colonial home, you're going to have a skewed perspective, and additionally you are at risk for losing a ton of equity. You will learn in this book that all real estate sales statistics, especially average sale prices, must be dissected and compared to the exact style/size/amenity-filled home you have.

5. Average Days on Market (DOM)

The average days on market is basically the statistic that measures how long a home is on the MLS until it receives a contract. This is important to realize. Most think it is the number that tells us how long it takes to sell a home. This is true, with one caveat, the average days on market represents **how long it takes to accept a contract from a home buyer**. While it does take a month or so to close on a sale, days on market tells us how long the home was on the market before a contract was accepted. So a home that is listed for sale on September 1st, and receives a contract from a home buyer on September 7th, was on the market for 7 days before accepting a contract. But the home doesn't see a closing table until November 1st. The days on market is still 7 days.

Nevertheless, days on market is a key metric that can tell us a story about how the market is performing. Remember the Hoosick Falls example? In 2016, the 39 homes that sold all took an average of 144 days to receive a contract. Compare that to a market like Latham, where in 2016, 195 homes sold within 12 months, all combining for an average days on market of just 44 days. That is almost 3x the amount of home sales completed in 100 days faster than Hoosick Falls.

Days on market is another inkling into the overall demand a market possesses. Homes that sell fast are usually located in high demand areas and are priced accordingly. And sometimes they are priced too low. Homes that take longer to sell are usually located in low demand areas or are overpriced. Even some homes fail to sell in the best performing markets of our region, and 99.9% of the time, price is the reason.

You may say that the next four statistical categories are a bit more obscure than the previous categories, however it takes more than just looking at basic statistics when it comes time to pricing a home. Finding the hidden value is possible when you dive deeper and figure out how and why one home sells for more than another.

This is especially true when two homes are virtually identical in size, layout and location. Going deeper could mean discovering the secret to making more money in the sale of your own home.

6. List Price vs. Sale Price ratio

The list price to sale price ratio is an important, in-depth statistic that is crucial to understand when it's time to price and sell your home. If you ask $250,000 for your home, and you receive an offer for $250,000, you have received 100% of your list price. This is better known as a full price offer.

But a more realistic example would be a home listed at $300,000. Let's say a home is on the market for three months and the seller has received no offers. The seller then drops the price to $275,000. Within days, the seller receives a full price offer of $275,000. In this case, while this is a 100% List Price to Sale Price result, we have to be aware that it is still 92% of the **original** asking price of $300,000. You will see many examples of where homes sitting on the market for months on end, sell in a matter of days, but only after they drop the price.

Either way, we want to be aware of how the local List Price vs. Sale Price statistic is performing in your area. Most homes in the Capital Region sell between 95% and 100% of asking price. This means that if your home has been on the market awhile and hasn't yet received a contract, then your asking price is too high. We know this because you have not received an offer between 95% and 100% of your asking price. Most home sellers think that the lower you drop your asking price, the lower the offer amounts will be. This is simply not true. With List Price vs. Sale Price statistics, we can see exactly what amount you can expect to receive for your home, but only when your asking price is accurate. The more accurate your asking price (List Price) is, the closer you will get to a 100% full price offer.

7. Absorption Rate

You have most likely never heard of absorption rate but it is, in fact, the number one factor for determining the health of the local real estate market. Calculating and referencing the local absorption rate is actually required by the Federal Housing Authority when bank appraisers are conducting an analysis for the bank during a real estate transaction. The absorption rate is often referred to as the months of supply. In other words, how long would it take all the current homes for sale on the market to sell out, if no other homes were to come onto the market at all?

A common theme of 2017 has been "low inventory". Of course, while a bit exaggerated to generate attention, low inventory (Supply) is good news for home sellers, especially where demand is high. The earmark for absorption rate is set at 6 months. Said differently, if I calculate your areas absorption rate to be less than 6 months, the market is favorable for home sellers. If it is longer than 6 months, the market is favoring home buyers. Absorption rate is simple really. It is calculated by taking the number of homes that have sold over the last 3 to 6 months and dividing them by the number of homes currently for sale.

For example, 100 homes have sold in the last 6 months in Clifton Park (not actual, just an example) that means 16.6 homes sell each month in Clifton Park. We then divide 16.6 by the amount of homes currently for sale on the market, let's say its 50 homes. We can then divide 16.6 and 50 both ways, to get two different metrics.

16.6 home sales per month / 50 homes currently for sale = 33% absorption rate

An absorption rate over 20% is considered a sellers' market, and will always equate to a number less than 6 months. We can also calculate this the other way.

50 homes for sale currently / 16.6 home sales per month = 3.01 months of supply.

Both numbers mean the same thing, which is, it's a sellers' market. And if zero homes were listed from here on out using this example, there would be no homes to choose from in just 3 months' time. Absorption rates are a key indicator into determining the Supply and Demand within your market. Absorption rate is like looking at a company's stock price, it fluctuates and moves with the market, but it also tells us a story.

8. **Price Per Square Foot**

This is actually one of the more common statistical categories, but surely can be easily overlooked. This stat is especially great when you begin to narrow down the market based on home styles and overall square footage. Of course thousands of homes sell each year in our area and a home's square footage can range from 500 square feet to 5,000 square feet. The price per square foot for a 1,800 square foot home will be different than the price per square foot of a 3,000 square foot home.

Price per square foot usually works in reverse. The smaller the home, usually the higher the price per square foot is. So let's say a 1,800 square foot Colonial home sold for $125 per square foot recently in your neighborhood. That would equate to $225,000 sale price. (1,800 x $125) But you know your home is around 2,700 square feet. Your price per square foot is going to be closer to $100, and not the $125. Even though your home is worth more, price per square foot decreases as the home size scales up. Price per square foot is determined when a home sells. Thus, when we list your home for sale, we want to be competitive with our price, and using the local price per square foot averages of home sales as our guide, can keep us competitive when it comes to pricing your home. Every day I see homes that fail to sell while on the market, and noticing their price per square foot is higher than the price per square foot of recent home sales means the home is overpriced and failing to entice an offer.

9. **Differential**

This may be talked about briefly throughout this book, so I will take the time to give you an example now. Differential is a very easy statistic to understand. It is basically the difference between the homes listed for sale and the number of homes sold. So what's different with this statistic compared to the sale percentage statistic? It tells us how big the gap is between the Supply and Demand of any market. We all know that from

2004 to 2007, the real estate market went from hot, to not. And what is fascinating about statistics is, just looking at the Differential can tell us how inflated, and fraudulent the real estate market was. Figure 1.2 shows the overall home sales within Albany County from 2006 to 2016. You will see the total differential in the right hand column which is calculated by subtracting the homes sold from the homes listed. More homes are always offered for sale than the amount of homes that end up selling. Notice how the differential goes from 89 in 2007 all the way to 1,302 in 2008. In Figure 1.2, we see what an oversupply of homes looks like in 2008. Supply skyrockets in 2008, but demand remains steady. See Figure 1.2 below.

Figure 1.2: Albany County overall home sales. 2006-2016

Year	Homes Listed	Homes Sold	Differential
2006	1773	1731	42
2007	1845	1756	**89**
2008	3115	1813	**1302**
2009	3215	1962	1253
2010	3427	1782	1645
2011	3331	1776	1555
2012	3397	1970	1427
2013	3632	2187	1445
2014	3681	2169	1512
2015	3930	2466	1464
2016	3731	2735	996

*Courtesy of the Eastern NY Multiple Listing Service from 1/1/2006 to 12/31/2016

We notice also how the market bounces back. Once the panic ensued, every home owner rushed to dump their home on the market. We see the amount of homes listed go from 1,845 to 3,115 from 2007 to 2008. Lucky for us here in the Capital Region, demand maintained. Notice how the number of homes sold still increased for three years from 2006-2009 before dipping a bit back into the 1,700 range. Even still, we see home sales climb right back again in 2012.

Since 2012, the Capital Region market has been healthy. It's ironic that homes listed for sale have never really stopped hitting the market since 2008.

Supply jumped so fast and has kept going here for ten years. While Demand is still catching up, it too has continued to grow. This is one of the reasons why the market could get even stronger in 2018. (This book was written in Fall of 2017). If Demand keeps up its pace and Supply suddenly dips back to the lower 3,000 range, we will definitely see home prices sky rocket to an absurd level. A level that's great for sellers but could be unaffordable for buyers. Thus, Supply and Demand will work out those kinks on its own.

Again, we cannot control what the market does, we can only learn about it and monitor it so that we can set you up for the most success when it comes time to sell.

This is what this book aims to enlighten you with. The reality of the real estate market. The market is alive and well, it has a pulse, and I have tapped into it. So, I'm glad you're here. I am also flattered and grateful that you have taken the time to read this book. I assure you the 5 Key Factors I am about to unveil will give you everything you need to make an informed decision when it comes to pricing and selling your home. Instead of boring you with just statistical information. I am going to use real examples from my experiences and home sales as a real estate broker here in the Capital Region of Albany, NY, as well as other in-depth information from the Capital Region's housing market which has never before been released to the public until now. Before we move onto Key Factor #1, I want to show you the Top 5 leaders in each of the 5 main statistical categories I study on the surface. This will give you an idea of where the most home buyer demand is in our region.

You'll see that in your own home sale, lining up the 5 Key Factors is all it takes to get the most money out of your home and defend your equity. Take a look at the Top 5 leaders in each real estate statistical category, through June 2017, on the next page.

Top 5 Leaders in Homes Listed For Sale through June 2017

1. Clifton Park: 435 Homes
2. Saratoga Springs: 414 Homes
3. Niskayuna: 400 Homes
4. Rotterdam (12306): 328 Homes
5. Scotia-Glenville: 324 Homes

Top 5 Leaders in Homes Sold through June 2017

1. Clifton Park: 277 Homes Sold
2. Niskayuna: 266 Homes Sold
3. Saratoga Springs: 259 Homes Sold
4. Ballston Spa: 202 Homes Sold
5. Scotia-Glenville: 195 Homes Sold

Top 5 Leaders in % of Listings Sold through June 2017

1. Delmar: 75%
2. Colonie: 74%
3. Latham: 73%
4. North Greenbush: 71%
5. Albany (12203): 70%

Top 5 Leaders in Average Sale Price through June 2017

1. Slingerlands: $407,154
2. Saratoga Springs: $387,395
3. Loudonville: $355,698
4. Ballston Lake: $320,524
5. Gansevoort: $294,490

Top 5 Leaders in Days on Market through June 2017

1. Delmar: 36 Days
2. Latham: 39 Days
3. Colonie: 44 Days
4. Loudonville: 45 Days
5. Ballston Spa: 49 Days

Courtesy of the Eastern NY Regional Multiple Listing Service from 1/1/2017 to 7/1/2017

It probably wasn't a shock to see some of the same towns and cities hitting the Top 5 in multiple categories. These numbers will continue to change, and by the end of the year, the final rankings will be in. But the point to realize is that the data tells us a story and it is also always telling the truth. We can trust the data to give us the accurate information on the real estate markets performance and analyzing this data is how we get the best overall sale prices for our clients. As they say, the numbers don't lie.

DEFEND YOUR EQUITY

KEY FACTOR #1: **LOCATION**

by Ryan Hoffman

We have all heard the adage; *"Location, Location, Location"*. Cliché and corny I know. But the one thing I have noticed about clichés is, they usually ring true. Due to their redundancy, they've lost their flare, and the meaning of the cliché itself is lost forever.

Ironically, the real estate practitioners of long ago coined this adage as an obvious point that we should not take with a grain of salt. Location is everything. I don't have to tell you that. Again, this is an obvious cliché we are talking about. But it must be dissected in order for the blinders to come off of home owners eyes. Location is a foundational pillar for the successful, and profitable, sale of your home, so let's see what location can do for your bottom line.

Ranking real estate markets is something that I started over three years ago. To be honest, I was kind of making things up as I went along, until I discovered how to use the statistical categories laid out in the previous chapter, to rank the towns and cities in our region in order from first, to last. In other words, my #1 ranked market, within the rankings, means high demand and leverage for home sellers.

Ranking the local zip codes and school districts in order of "leverage", or better yet, demand, was done by using a simple algorithm.

Each Sunday, I continue to populate the weekly housing sales data into my database. New homes hit the market, homes sell, and with that comes all of the other information within this data that tells us a story. This "story" comes from the statistical categories I discussed in the introduction that include the number of **homes listed, homes sold**, the **percentage of homes sold, average sale prices, days on market**, and so on.

Points are awarded based on a market's performance within all these categories and the total points are added up at the end. Once the points are totaled we can then see who has scored the most points, and who has scored the least points. The highest scores represent the healthiest real estate markets in our area that are favorable to home sellers. When the rankings shake out, in order from #1 to #70, it tells us a story that we really cannot be surprised with. It shows us a ranked list of the highest demand, most popular, easiest to sell, real estate markets in our region.

On the following page, you will see a sample of what the Top 10 markets look like at the midway point of 2017, right here in the Capital Region.

Top Ranked Zip Codes in the Capital Region: Mid-Year 2017

Based on Ryan Hoffman's Real Estate Index Ranking System

1. Saratoga Springs, 12866
2. Clifton Park, 12065
3. Ballston Spa, 12020
4. Ballston Lake, 12019
5. Colonie, 12205
6. Loudonville, 12211
7. Delmar, 12054
8. Latham, 12110
9. Albany, 12203 (Western Ave area)
10. Niskayuna, 12309

Are we really surprised when we see this list? Are we really surprised to learn that these 10 zip code markets continuously score the highest points in: **Homes Listed, Homes Sold, Sale Percentage, Days on Market, Average Sale Price**, and other in-depth statistical categories?

This list tells us where it is the easiest to sell a home. If your home is located within one of these top 10 zip codes, things are looking good for your ability to attract a lot of home buyers and make more money in the sale.

I don't want to get you too confused and sidetracked, I know this is Key Factor #1: Location. But it was important to point out these Power Rankings as a guide to rank the best markets in our area. It's an important starting point for your home sale and also a great look at why these areas are ranked in the Top 10.

Look at the Top 4 zip code markets for example. They are all located in Saratoga County. Does this really surprise us? It shouldn't. And the fact that I used statistical analysis and a simple algorithm to put it all together, rather than my opinion, makes me feel that it is an accurate depiction of the local real estate market. Especially since I can compare it to what I already know about these areas. If the #1 market in my rankings ended up being Rotterdam, for instance, this wouldn't make much sense to me.

Anyone that lives in our area already knows that Clifton Park, Saratoga, and other Saratoga County locations are some of the most popular and desirable places to live. So the fact that my real estate rankings have awarded these locations the top spots within the rankings, further verifies the point that Supply and Demand rules the sale of your home and location has a lot to do with it. So let's take a few zip codes and talk about their overall ranking, but with a special focus on their geographic location.

Out of the Top 10 zip code markets, four are located in Saratoga County. And not just 4 out of 10, but the Top 4. And it all makes sense to me. #1 Saratoga Springs is *always* the place to be, in a sense, not just the "Summer place to be". The quaint downtown and seemingly healthy economy, make it one of the few classic cities that have sustained in our area, and in the country, over time. Most old downtown city atmospheres have gone by the wayside, but not Saratoga, of course the Racetrack is a big part of it, but that adds even more to the point. Would it surprise you to learn the average sale price in Saratoga Springs (12866) is just under $400,000?

Figure 1.3: 12866 Saratoga Real Estate Stats Mid-Year 2017

Listed	Sold	% Sold	Avg $	DOM
414	259	63%	$387,395	65

Courtesy of the Eastern NY Regional Multiple Listing Service from 1/1/2017 to 7/1/2017

Obviously it's no surprise. Anyone familiar with Saratoga Springs thinks about the affluence that comes along with this city, and sale prices back up that perception. So what about the other Saratoga County areas that rank in the Top 4?

Clifton Park (12065), at the time of this writing, was gaining a bit of ground on Saratoga Springs, in an effort to take over as the #1 real estate market. And I expect them to be #1 by years end. Only because they have been #1 for more than a decade. They have always, in my analysis, been the #1 real estate market in the four main counties of our region. If anyone needs to "defend their equity" in the Capital Region, it is the home owners in the 12065 zip code.

So why do you think that is? Well, for Key Factor #1 - Location, Clifton Park offers the best of both worlds. Easy access to Saratoga and all points North, plus, a somewhat tolerable commute to Albany and other desirable locations in Albany and Rensselaer counties. Yes I know, the dreaded Northway traffic. But the fact that folks are willing to tolerate the white-knuckle, stressful and frustrating commute from Clifton Park to Albany or their workplace in Albany County presumably, regardless of this traffic, tells us what a desirable location is worth to them. And not only do folks tolerate it once a day, but twice a day, every day, five days a week, 52 weeks a year.

This is the sacrifice they make to live in a great, centralized location. People's behavior and the real estate market statistics, can tell us all we need to know about where demand lies, and it starts with location.

Figure 1.4: 12065 Clifton Park Real Estate Stats Mid-Year 2017

Listed	Sold	% Sold	Avg $	DOM
435	277	64%	$284,598	50

Courtesy of the Eastern NY Regional Multiple Listing Service from 1/1/2017 to 7/1/2017

When looking at Figure 1.4, it tells us that Clifton Park is a top area when it comes to housing volume. Clifton Park is on pace to list around 800 homes for sale this year. When sale percentages push 70% success, with days on market (DOM) at just 50 days for Clifton Park, we see the data backs up the fact that this is an ideal location for Capital Region folks and tells us there is high demand.

The other two Saratoga County zip codes of Ballston Spa, 12020 and Ballston Lake, 12019 share the same affinity with folks in Clifton Park and Saratoga. These other two top markets are again, close to Saratoga, all points North, and are located in a great setting usually consisting of planned developed neighborhoods, good schools and for the moment, decent taxes. Yes the dreaded tax word. We will be getting to taxes and schools here soon.

Of course there are other great reasons to live in all these areas, but I am here to simply point out the few that can be somewhat measured to prove location is key and a cliché that is all but dead.

The rest of the Top 10 markets are left to Albany County, with only one, Niskayuna, located in the Schenectady County market. Figure 1.5

shows us 5th ranked Colonie, the 12205 zip code, and their real estate stats at the halfway point of 2017.

Figure 1.5: 12205 Colonie Real Estate Stats Mid-Year 2017

Listed	Sold	% Sold	Avg $	DOM
202	149	74%	$199,402	44

Courtesy of the Eastern NY Regional Multiple Listing Service from 1/1/2017 to 7/1/2017

As we saw in my rankings on page 23, we end up with Colonie, the 12205 zip code, as the 5th overall best real estate market in our region. While there are other factors at play here, what Colonie really has going for it is the prime location. The 12205 zip code spans up and down Central Avenue and Sand Creek Road, stretching from the Everett Road area, all the way up to the Schenectady County line.

With obvious access to all points within the region, it is no surprise why Colonie is ranked 5th best among all real estate markets. Getting to downtown Albany, the City of Schenectady, all points North on Interstate 87, and also close access to Interstate 90, it has everything a human needs for a convenient lifestyle. Wolf Road and Central Avenue have all the shops and restaurants you could imagine when living in that immediate area, including Trader Joes.

2017 is proving to be a great year for Colonie. With homes, at the time of this writing, getting offers within just 44 days on the market, sale prices remain affordable hovering around $200,000, with 202 homes listed by mid-year.

Remember what I said about demand keeping up with supply? No matter the market, big or small, a simple look at Homes Listed versus

Homes Sold tells us all we need to know about home buyer demand. 74% of homes are selling in Colonie this year. That is a very, very healthy market. And with its great location, home owners are reaping the rewards when selling.

I want to point out two other stellar real estate markets and the unbelievable year they are having in 2017. Staying in Albany County, the little hamlet of Latham is a dominating real estate market in 2017 (and usually any year really) and the geographic location, among other factors, is the reason why. Figure 1.6 shows us how home sales were performing in the middle of 2017.

Figure 1.6: 12110 Latham Real Estate Stats Mid-Year 2017

Listed	Sold	% Sold	Avg $	DOM
131	95	73%	$245,284	39

Courtesy of the Eastern NY Regional Multiple Listing Service from 1/1/2017 to 7/1/2017

On average, a home is lasting just 39 days on the market in Latham, so home buyers better be on their toes. You'll notice that Latham, differs greatly, in the amount of available houses for sale on the market, when compared to a bigger zip code such as Clifton Park. Regardless of having lower volume, Latham can still rank as a Top 10 market due to their performance in the main statistical categories.

Latham home owners have a lot to be excited about. Whether they are selling now, or into 2018, things are looking really good for this small town that has location, and all the amenities, going for it. Latham boasts every commercial store you could think of, in many different retail categories, from home improvement, to discount supercenters, arts and craft stores, clothing and more. There are plenty of corporate and private restaurants, and overall, Latham is basically the bullseye to all points located in the Capital Region. In all four directions, Latham can get you to Saratoga, Troy, Schenectady and Albany, within 30 minutes or less. Latham really has it all, and the statistics back that up. 39 days on market? Wow. What real estate market could even come close to that speed of sale? How about Delmar?

The 12054 zip code is a similar size to Latham, and boy does it pack a punch. Home buyers again, need to bring their A-game and they better come packing with good mortgage terms versus other home buyers in this market. Compared to other top real estate markets, Delmar does not produce a lot of volume, and with few homes to choose from, home buyer competition is fierce. Let's take a look at Delmar's real estate market performance so far this year in 2017. See Figure 1.7 below.

Figure 1.7: 12054 Delmar Real Estate Stats Mid-Year 2017

Listed	Sold	% Sold	Avg $	DOM
156	117	75%	$271,505	36

Courtesy of the Eastern NY Regional Multiple Listing Service from 1/1/2017 to 7/1/2017

Whoa, what's this? 36 days on the market, on average, before a home buyer offers on a home for sale in Delmar, NY? If you hadn't guessed, Delmar is one of the fastest moving markets in the region this year. And it's the location that can be counted on to provide us some insight into its peak performance.

An obvious point here is the fact that Delmar is *the* premier Albany suburb. Not only is it right on top of the City of Albany, but it is also a small, quaint little town, where folks are proud to live, and classic home styles are abound. Being on top of Albany is an obvious reason why

Delmar is so sought after. And with easy-on-easy-off access to Route 85, Interstate 90 and 787, Delmar provides that convenient location with classic charm, and a bit of affluence to go with it.

Average sale prices are slowly eyeing that $300,000 mark, and you shouldn't be shocked to see quite a handful of homes sell for well over $300,000 in the Delmar zip code.

Delmar will most likely end up as a Top 5 market by years end, and even with just 117 homes sold at the mid-year point, this is a very strong market that is appealing to home buyers and profitable for home sellers.

The outskirts

I think it's important to drive the location point home by ending our talk on the #1 Key Factor, with some cities and towns you may or may not be familiar with.

There are many areas of our region where I do not practice real estate in, mainly due to their location. But looking at how great some of these top real estate markets are performing is worth a lot more when you take the comparison approach. When looking at a few markets that aren't performing well, we find the main reason for their inconsistence is due to their inconvenient location. See Figure 1.8 below.

Figure 1.8: 12123 Nassau Real Estate Stats Mid-Year 2017

Listed	Sold	% Sold	Avg $	DOM
46	19	41%	$173,825	83

Courtesy of the Eastern NY Regional Multiple Listing Service from 1/1/2017 to 7/1/2017

Nassau, the 12123 zip code, sits on the southeastern edge of Rensselaer County. Some homes pull from the East Greenbush School District thus helping their average sale price. But even with just 46 listings, only 19 have sold, and those took an average of 83 days on the market to do so. Nassau is a good 30 minute commute to Albany, not too bad. But otherwise, all points North, South and East, is desolate country side with not much to offer, unless of course you are looking for that kind of lifestyle.

Another example of how a desolate geographic location can be compared with the real estate data is the 12143 zip code of Ravena. Ravena may be more recognizable to you, but of course, being south of Albany by 30+ minutes, and bordering the Thruway, there isn't much convenience for living in the Ravena area. Long commutes and few amenities, have definitely affected its housing market.

Figure 1.9 below shows us real estate stats in the 12143 zip code through the first half of 2017.

Figure 1.9: 12143 Ravena Real Estate Stats Mid-Year 2017

Listed	Sold	% Sold	Avg $	DOM
38	19	50%	$154,843	107

Courtesy of the Eastern NY Regional Multiple Listing Service from 1/1/2017 to 7/1/2017

The 19 home sales took over three months to sell on average, and even with low supply, there is not much demand there in Ravena. Home sellers have a 50-50 shot of selling their home, and need to price it attractively in an effort to sell it for the best market value without a whole lot of stress. Home buyers have the upper hand in Ravena, with absorption rates well over 10 months, home sellers are left without many cards in their hand and better jump on any buyer that shows interest.

Two examples of low demand areas is enough for you to get the picture, I'm sure. When we think of location as the #1 Key Factor, the statistics back us up on what we already know geographically. Good locations, are usually, good performing real estate markets. And desolate locations, offer less to home buyers and make it harder to sell for home owners.

But even after seeing how Clifton Park, Latham and Delmar are performing in comparison to Nassau and Ravena, does that mean that real estate agents in the Top 5 areas are good, and the real estate agents in the low ranked areas are bad? Of course this makes no sense. Which is more proof that the market, not the agent, determine your home sale.

The reason for the ranking system, and all the analysis I do, as outlined in this book, is to see who has control within the market. Ravena and Nassau are not bad areas to live, and I am not trying to call them out in a negative way. In fact, there are dozens of other markets in the region where home demand is low due to an inconvenient location and in addition to the other key factors. What I am trying to convey is that a home seller in Ravena, needs to put their emotional attachments for their home, and the perception of value they may have, on the sidelines, and let the market tell them where they stand based on the factors explained in this book.

When you own a home in a top demand market and have a great location, you are in the driver's seat. In some cases, home buyers will fight over your home, so understanding your position based on market data and recent market performance, takes precedence over personal feelings and opinions.

Location has long been the go-to adage for the marketing of real estate. It is also a factor that will never change, that is unless, an entire market changes over time. Obviously it can happen. Over time generations move and cities and towns can change. Some for the better, others for the worse. We all know of those cities and towns in our local area that used to be bustling, but have since lost their appeal.

Usually, it takes a long time for trends to swing in real estate, no matter how good or bad. Demand just won't disappear overnight in your town and you also cannot expect to make an extra $50,000 on your home in just 12 months either. Although both are possible, it's usually indicative of a crisis or a real estate bubble.

Following the market in close detail is the best way to be an informed home seller and feel confident that your home is worth the price you have determined based on the data. Since real estate practitioners usually keep this data under lock and key, you're left to seek your own public devices for determining home value, which can be a time consuming and frustrating task to tackle.

Well, it doesn't end with just a prime location. What else does your home have going for it? No, I'm not talking about your new countertops, although, those will matter. Before we get busy dissecting the inner workings and perks inside your home, let's stay outside the box for now, and head into Key Factor #2; School Districts.

I should note that, like the zip code markets I have talked about and ranked in order of buyer demand, it is important to realize that there are really two separate rankings within the real estate market that I have created based on data. Location is directly tied into School District, and for good reason.

There are a lot of zip codes that pull from various school districts, and this fact alone can have a big impact on a home seller's bottom line. A lot of zip code markets, such as Clifton Park, 12065, pulls from one school district; Shenendehowa. This makes things easy because when we are talking about how good the Clifton Park market is, we are also saying how good the Shenendehowa Schools District is.

For other areas, we will see how the difference in school district, even while in the same zip code, can affect average sale prices and other statistical performances, by a big margin. This helps us shed light even further on demand, and how to understand your homes position within the local real estate market.

KEY FACTOR #2: **SCHOOL DISTRICT**

by Ryan Hoffman

Schools matter. A lot. When I first started analyzing the real estate market years ago, I focused my research solely on zip code boundaries. I had soon learned that it wasn't enough. School districts weigh heavily on the sale of your home, and they also determine how much money your home is worth to interested home buyers. The real estate data within the school districts themselves had to be dissected and the results from this research was astonishing.

School Districts are important for obvious reasons. Parents want their children to grow up in a "good school district". This is usually perceived based on multiple factors such as test scores, graduation rates, experiences by students and parents, and of course public perception. But I have noticed that authority web sites are sparse when it comes to the subject of ranking school districts. For me, the solution was simple, the real estate data based on the school district can tell us how popular a school district is. Ranking the districts in order of demand can uncover information about local home buyer behavior.

The way I see it, school districts can be ranked based on the real estate sales and data within the districts themselves. Without a true power authority for accurately ranking school districts, I feel that using the real estate sales data, with the same statistical categories and ranking system I use for zip codes, can prove that demand for one school district versus another can be uncovered using the real estate market as our guide.

Just as I used multiple statistical categories to rank zip code markets, I use the same categories to rank the most in-demand school districts. And also, just like the zip code markets, I think you'd agree that one look at the Top 10 school districts in my rankings will verify what we already know to be true. Close your eyes and think about the school district your home pulls from. And also think about what you perceive to be the best schools in our area.

Now look at my rankings on the next page of the Top 10 School Districts. Do you see any similarities in my rankings when compared to your own knowledge and opinion of the school districts in our local area?

Top Ranked School Districts in the Capital Region: Mid-Year 2017

Based on Ryan Hoffman's Real Estate Index Ranking System

1. **Shenendehowa**
2. **Guilderland**
3. **North Colonie**
4. **South Colonie**
5. **Ballston Spa**
6. **Bethlehem**
7. **Saratoga Springs**
8. **Niskayuna**
9. **Burnt Hills-Ballston Lake**
10. **East Greenbush**

Do these rankings surprise you? Probably not. And you may even be thinking that these rankings aren't so prolific after all. Keep in mind, that these school district rankings are based off of the school districts performance in the various real estate statistical categories that I use.

The list you're seeing is a culmination of the school districts where homes sell the fastest, sell for the most money, and where sales are matching up with supply. Apart from that, my experience within the market, working with both buyers and sellers, has proven these rankings to be pretty accurate and important based on consumer desires.

Buying a home inside the Shenendehowa School District is a big goal for a lot of home buyers. Combine the desirable location of Clifton Park, with that of a desirable school district, and we are on our way to discovering how these factors lead to, not only the sale of real estate, but how it equates to home buyers competing to give sellers the most money for their home. I am using Shenendehowa as an example because my experience within this market has consisted of my home buying clients losing out on homes to competing buyers, and my home selling clients getting a lot of attention on their home and seeing it sell quickly, usually having to choose from multiple offers. So of course, after ranking the school districts based on the real estate sales statistics, the rankings end up telling the truth about what the demand is for these areas.

I am sure you're thinking that since Shenendehowa is the only school district to pull from the Clifton Park zip code, that by default, the statistics are the same as the zip code statistics and common sense says that these findings are of no surprise. While there is a bit of truth to that thought process, it is not that cut and dry.

The reason being that while Clifton Park and the 12065 zip code only pulls in one school district, (Shenendehowa), the school district of Shenendehowa itself pulls in **six different zip codes**. When you begin to drill down deeper into this concept, you realize that demand, sale prices, swiftness of sale, and other outcomes, change based on the school district your home pulls from, regardless if you're in a top performing zip code or not. Let's use data from 2016, to give you a visual on how the real estate market data can continuously tell us a story time and time again. For this example, let's get outside Saratoga County for a moment.

Let's use the City of Watervliet and the 12189 zip code for my next point. It takes just one look at the data to know that Watervliet is not a high demand real estate market. While it does have some things going for it, the data proves that the 12189 zip code isn't at the top of a home buyers shopping list. Let's take a look at the housing market statistics Watervliet has posted for the year 2016. Figure 2.1, on the next page, will give us an easier example to understand when looking at a full year.

Figure 2.1: 12189 (Watervliet) Real Estate Stats. End of 2016

Listed	Sold	% Sold	Avg $	DOM
162	109	67%	$174,283	58

Courtesy of the Eastern NY Regional Multiple Listing Service from 1/1/2016 to 12/31/2016

The Watervliet zip code of 12189 isn't a high powered real estate market. Ranked #42 overall out of the 70 zip codes I track, we see that it took around 60 days to sell a home in 2016, with almost a 70% chance of success. Not too bad for the 42nd ranked market overall. Average sale prices flirting with $175,000 seems a bit high for Watervliet, and even with these stats, they hadn't really scored enough points to move up in the rankings.

"But Ryan, I thought we were talking about school districts here, this is the Watervliet zip code!"

Based on my experience within the real estate industry, and the Capital Region, I was often confused on why Watervliet's numbers were a bit deceiving. With a 67% sale success rate and a decent days on market, it felt like the 12189 zip code was over performing. This didn't seem right until I discovered that it was because of the school districts that are inside the 12189 zip code. While 12189 is the zip code and mailing address for many people in Watervliet, not all houses contain residents inside the City of Watervliet, nor are they pulling from the Watervliet City School District.

So what's going on here?

Zip Code boundaries are really used for the United States Postal Service, and everything from real estate data, and other demographic data, can be easily organized by the use of zip code boundaries. Heck, it seems easy enough. Pull a list of all home sales in 12189 and we have a clear picture of the real estate market, right? Not so fast.

The 12189 zip code pulls from two very different school districts.

1. Watervliet City School District

2. North Colonie School District

This is why segmentation is key. To a first-time home buyer, or even a non-savvy real estate agent, when they hear, or see, Watervliet attached to an address, they immediately judge it as being undesirable when compared to other locations in our region. They may also see a home for sale with a 12189 mailing address and compare that to the asking price, and think; "They want how much for this Watervliet home?"

But it is the school district that needs to be pointed out and used to justify the desirability of the home, and it's asking price. It is the opinion of many locals, that the North Colonie School District is very desirable, with Shaker being a highly touted high school in our area. Remember how North Colonie School District is ranked 3rd overall in our School District Rankings? (Page 37) Let's take the 12189 zip code statistics from 2016 and **segment them by the school district** and see what the differences are. See Figure 2.2 and Figure 2.3 on the following page.

Figure 2.2: 12189 Home Sales + Watervliet Schools: 2016

Listed	Sold	% Sold	Avg $	DOM
80	54	68%	$114,089	67

Courtesy of the Eastern NY Regional Multiple Listing Service from 1/1/2016 to 7/1/2016

Figure 2.3: 12189 Home Sales + North Colonie Schools: 2016

Listed	Sold	% Sold	Avg $	DOM
81	54	67%	$234,476	48

Courtesy of the Eastern NY Regional Multiple Listing Service from 1/1/2016 to 7/1/2016

This is really one of the best examples of segmenting school districts inside a zip code that you will see. Folks that sold a home in 12189, and pulled from the North Colonie School District made an extra **$120,000** in the sale of their home versus home sales within the Watervliet School District. It's safe to say that school districts matter.

One of the best reasons why this example paints a good picture of the importance of school districts, is because the overall sales inside the two school districts are practically identical. When split by school district, each set of data inside the 12189 zip code presents a good visual to easily see the discernable difference and weight that a school district has. 80 homes listed for sale inside the Watervliet School District to go along with 54 sales, and 81 homes listed for sale in North Colonie District, with

54 sales, **both inside the same zip code of 12189**. It cannot get much closer than this.

On the surface, when looking at the stats of the 12189 (Figure 2.1, page 39) zip code, we think that average sale prices are around $175,000. But if your home is in the 12189 zip code **and** pulls from Watervliet Schools, the real average sale price you should be looking at is $114,089 (Figure 2.2, page 41). The stats of the zip code aren't enough. **We must always drill down into the separate school districts that are inside the zip code because the overall zip code averages are not painting a true picture of the market.**

I touched on the fact that North Colonie Schools ranked 3rd overall in my school district rankings, and the 12110 zip code of Latham ranked 8th overall in the zip code rankings. The reasons why the Latham zip code doesn't rank as high as the North Colonie School District is because of the other zip codes that also pull from the North Colonie School District.

This can be said about a lot of local markets. Yes, the 12110 Latham zip code, and all its home owners, only have one school district to worry about. But the North Colonie School District pulls in 5 zip codes by itself, beyond just the 12110 Latham zip code. These additional zip codes are:

12047, Cohoes
12211, Loudonville
12204, Menands
12189, Watervliet
12110, Latham

When I pull school district statistics and rank these districts in order of demand, I am pulling in data from all the zip codes that these districts cover. On the zip code side, we are pulling in all data from that zip code, which includes multiple school districts for the majority of markets. This is why having two sets of rankings, **Zip Codes and School Districts** is crucial in an effort to see the true story within your market. It is also the reason why the rankings will be similar, but not an exact mirror image of each other.

Let's take a look at the five zip codes inside the North Colonie School District and compare their performances at the halfway point of 2017. The table below shows all the zip code markets in the North Colonie School District and their real estate statistics thus far, sorted by the number of homes listed for sale, with Latham showing the most listings.

Figure 2.4: North Colonie Schools: Housing Stats by Zip Code Mid 2017

Zip Code	Listed	Sold	% Sold	Avg $	DOM
Latham 12110	158	107	68%	$245,905	37
Loudonville 12211	109	60	55%	$393,475	46
Watervliet 12189	56	37	66%	$269,155	52
Cohoes 12047	35	12	34%	$357,191	41
Menands 12204	23	10	44%	$371,867	60

*Courtesy of the Eastern NY Regional Multiple Listing Service from 1/1/2017 to 7/1/2017

You wouldn't think that homes located in the Cohoes zip code, or even Menands zip code, are selling for over $350,000. If we looked at the zip code stats first, we would see average sale prices below $200,000. This is why, again, segmenting is so important. But because of the school district they are pulling from, zip codes take a back seat on the overall performance these homes have in the market. As I touched on before, the statistics can be deceiving if we didn't drill down and look further into the key factor of school districts. With Watervliet home owners as the example, one look at the average sale price of $175,000, in the 12189 zip code, is enough to get them excited. But when we looked at the two different school districts contributing to the zip code totals, we see the 12189 averages were inflated due to North Colonie School Districts peak performance. Watervliet home sellers should be looking at the average sale price in the $114,000 range so not to be misled. (Figure 2.2 Page 41)

So what about that same scenario in Shenendehowa schools? I am going to use the year 2016 as the example here since it's a full year of data in the books. Figure 2.5 will give you a clear picture on the entire calendar year when it comes to this school districts performance in the real estate market.

Figure 2.5: Shenendehowa School District Final Stats: 2016

Listed	Sold	% Sold	Avg $	DOM
967	776	71%	$291,086	53

Courtesy of the Eastern NY Regional Multiple Listing Service from 1/1/2016 to 12/31/2016

Wow, a 71% sale success rate for Shenendehowa home sellers in all of 2016. The average sale prices were close to that $300,000 mark and homes were selling in just 53 days on average. Things were looking really good for Shenendehowa home sellers in 2016, as they usually do? Right? Yes and No.

Obviously these are very powerful numbers and more justification of why the Shenendehowa School District is #1 on my list of the 49 School Districts I rank.

If I own a home inside the Shenendehowa School District, I definitely have leverage as a home seller. My home is located in the #1 school district, in an obvious sellers' market, so I may begin to think about pricing my home in the $250,000 - $300,000 range. This is where in-depth research helps home sellers understand what they really possess and how they can sell their home fast for the best possible price.

So you own a home that is inside the Shenendehowa School District, but what zip code are you in? Let's drill down the Shenendehowa home sale statistics and see the six zip codes they pull from and the differences that this makes in the overall sale prices, sale success, and time spent on the market.

Take a look at Figure 2.6 on the next page to see the Shenendehowa School District sales segmented by the zip codes that are inside the school district. The table is arranged in order of the amount of homes listed for sale. Of course we will see that the 12065 zip code boasts the largest amount of inventory inside the Shenendehowa School District at 607 homes listed for sale in all of 2016, followed by the Ballston Lake zip code of 12019 with 147 homes listed in 2016.

Now we can see where all of the home sales, within the Shenendehowa School District, took place, since I have segmented the home sales by zip code.

Figure 2.6: Shenedehowa Schools: Stats by Zip Code 2016:

Zip Code	Listed	Sold	% Sold	Avg $	DOM
Clifton Park 12065	605	509	84%	$270,600	46
Ballston Lake 12019	147	125	85%	$304,412	47
Waterford 12188	64	49	77%	$256,151	51
Mechanicville 12118	68	47	69%	382,544	94
Rexford 12148	63	35	56%	$340,648	33
Round Lake 12151	20	11	55%	$192,158	46

Courtesy of the Eastern NY Regional Multiple Listing Service from 1/1/2016 to 12/31/2016

We must always go deeper and segment the data by the zip codes within the school district. Round Lake sellers would be hard pressed to get $300,000 for their home, but they may believe they could when just looking at the average sale price for all of the Shenendehowa School District home sales. Instead, we see the average sale price for Round Lake homes, inside Shenendehowa schools, at just under $200,000. This is the information that is needed to make the correct pricing decision. If we did not segment and look deeper, a Round Lake seller may overprice their home and find themselves sitting on the market to no end.

But going in-depth is key to helping home sellers, and even buyers, understand what they are up against in the specific real estate market they are in. Who has the upper hand in the transaction? The buyer or the seller? When you possess something that home buyers demand, you have leverage, and you better use it to make sure you get the most money out of the sale of your home.

Again, we see homes inside zip codes like Waterford and Mechanicville (Figure 2.6) performing very well and much higher than they usually would, due to their Shenendehowa School District designation. Home sellers are being generously rewarded when it comes time to sell within this school district, getting more money for their home than what they could expect if not pulling from the Shenendehowa School District.

For example, home sales data in the 12118 zip code of Mechanicville, when combined with the Mechanicville School District shows a big difference when compared to the 47 homes that sold in the 12118 zip code, **and** pulled from Shenendehowa Schools, sold for, on average, $382,544. (Figure 2.6 on page 46) That's a great average sale price. But how did the 12118 zip code home sellers, who pull from the Mechanicville School District fare in the sale of their home? Take a look Figure 2.7 on the next page to see the results.

Figure 2.7: 12118 Home Sales in Mechanicville Schools 2016

Listed	Sold	% Sold	Avg $	DOM
128	65	51%	$211,992	49

Courtesy of the Eastern NY Regional Multiple Listing Service from 1/1/2016 to 12/31/2016

A bit of a difference wouldn't you say? Those who were lucky enough to have a Mechanicville address of 12118, **and** pull from Shenendehowa schools, saw an average sale price of **$170,000 more**, than those 12118 home sellers that had Mechanicville as their school district. That is a profound difference, to say the least.

Again, there is nothing wrong with Mechanicville schools. I am never trying to knock any area or school district when I make comparisons in this book. But again, "the numbers don't lie" as they say. Statistics are irrefutable evidence, not opinion. This process of segmenting data, and drilling down into the market, could even be considered a scientific approach to selling your home. The numbers tell us where home buyers are willing to pay more for a home, and that is important to know. Pricing your home accurately means everything when you decide to sell your home. It's one thing to have something of high demand, like a home in Clifton Park and the Shenendehowa School District. But arriving at the right price will not only determine how much money you make in the sale, it will also determine if any money was left behind at the closing table.

This data basically paints a picture of **what home buyers want**. The same home buyers you need to sell your home. The real estate industry trains agents on how to win your business, they do not teach pricing strategey. But you need to net the most money in your home sale and understanding the market, and using a pricing strategy, driven by market data, is the key.

With still three key factors to go, I think you'll agree that the sale of your home is determined on such factors. Using the key factors will have you better prepared to make empowered decisions as a home seller who needs to protect their biggest investment.

If you hadn't already looked ahead through this book, you may not be in total disbelief of Key Factor #3. After all, it's the only thing certain in life besides the certainty of death.

DEFEND YOUR EQUITY

KEY FACTOR #3: **TAXES**

By Ryan Hoffman

Taxes. I'm sure you're hoping this is a quick chapter. I mean, who wants to talk about the taxes we pay, let alone read an entire chapter on the subject? But when it comes to real estate, taxes are Key Factor #3.

As I am sure you are aware, the overall taxes you pay on your home (property and school) directly affect your monthly mortgage payment. Regardless if maybe you're reading this book and your mortgage is paid off, well then congratulations is surely in order. You've achieved something that 70% of America home owners will probably never achieve.

Understanding how your overall taxes are directly related to and in sync with your sale price is crucial for knowing your position in the marketplace. *Know your position?* What do I mean exactly when I say this?

It means, what does your home have going for it, or in it, that no other home in your neighborhood has?

Said differently; **why should I, a home buyer, buy your home, over all the other similar homes at similar prices in the same neighborhood that are on the market?**

This is a really hard question to answer, yet vital, because if you don't know the answer to this question, it could cost you a lot of money in end. I know this chapter is about your overall taxes affecting your sale, and I am getting to that… I am sure you're trying to contain your excitement.

Knowing your position in the local real estate market means coming to an understanding that you have accepted, about what your house has going for it. What are the benefits to buying your home? Understanding this will get you the most money in the sale because there will be no surprises. We know what to expect once we hit the "on" button and broadcast your home out to home buyers everywhere.

If we ignore just one key factor, or important detail, it could mean the worst case scenario for your home sale. And that's lost time, a lot of price reductions, and lost money.

No matter how mundane, overall taxes are a big part of the equation. And through statistics and data analysis, I think I have a pretty good way of showing you how home sellers, with low (lower than average) property taxes, are making more money from their homes than they probably ever imagined.

In 2016, 433 homes sold in the South Colonie School District. The average sale price of all 433 homes was $199,685. When averaging the tax amounts from each sale indicated on the Multiple Listing Service, the average tax amount paid per owner was $4,115 per year. Figure 3.1 puts this into perspective for us.

Figure 3.1: South Colonie School District Sales: Final 2016

# of Home Sales	Avg Sale Price	Avg. Tax Amount
433	$199,685	$4,115

*Courtesy of the Eastern NY Regional Multiple Listing Service from 1/1/2016 to 12/31/2016

This is one of the best school districts you can find that has some of the lowest taxes in our region. The reason I pull school districts when conducting this research is due to the overall school taxes home owners pay, which is usually much higher than the property tax amounts. It's important to indicate that the integrity of this information comes with an asterisk alongside it. Unfortunately, some real estate agents do not verify the correct tax amounts, and/or, they quote the tax amounts in the Multiple Listing Service that are much lower than the new buyer can expect to pay.

Home buyers frequently ask if the tax amounts are correct compared to the quote they see online. Heck, even real estate agents ask me if the tax amounts are correct when inquiring on my own listings. This is all due to the tax amounts consistently being miss-quoted by agents on their listings in the MLS.

One reason some agents do this is for marketability. If your overall tax amounts are $6,000 per year, but you have the STAR discount, plus a Veterans discount, you're paying approximately $4,500 per year. Not too bad. But this is not the amount the new buyer will pay. They can expect to dish out $6,000 per year from the very onset as the new owner, regardless if they are a military vet, or apply for STAR after the purchase is closed.

It's much more appealing to a home buyer to see a low tax amount on the property listing, for obvious reasons. Taxes are in the front of home buyer minds, since, it affects the monthly mortgage payment greatly.

When I talk about the average tax amounts here, such as the low taxes paid by South Colonie School District home owners, it deserves that asterisk due to lack of due diligence from some agents. Whatever the home seller tells their agent they pay, even if it's lower than a new buyer can expect, that tax amount is thrown onto the listing without a second thought from the agent. Bottom line is, quoting an overall tax amount that is much lower than what the new home buyer will have to pay, is not a sound strategy and causes nothing but headaches in the end.

With all this being said, the tax amounts talked about in this chapter, quoted from the Multiple Listing Service, are within the ball park of what home buyers can expect to pay.

We all know that the South Colonie area carries a reputation of having low taxes, and this leads to higher sale prices.

The reason why taxes is Key Factor #3 is due to its direct impact on home sale prices. Typically, the higher the overall tax amounts, the lower the sale price and, of course, vice versa. The lower the tax amounts on a property, this usually leads to a higher sale price.

Let's stick with South Colonie to further this point on property taxes. As mentioned, in the 2016 calendar year 433 homes sold within the South Colonie School District. The average sale price for all sales came to $199,685, with average total tax amounts per home coming in at just $4,115 per year.

What is important to realize here is that the South Colonie School District is comprised of mostly Ranch style homes. These home styles dominate the landscape. And most of these Ranch style homes are only 3 bedrooms. Yes, there are 4 bedroom Ranch homes, 2 bedroom Ranch homes, Cape Cod style homes, Raised Ranch, and so on, but the most common home that sells in South Colonie is a 3 bedroom 1 bathroom Ranch home.

In fact, of the 433 home sales in 2016 for South Colonie School District sellers, 146 of those home sales were Ranch style. The next closest sum of home styles came from Cape Code style homes at 65 total sales. And we can drill down even deeper than this. Of the 146 Ranch style sales, as I guessed, 97 were 3 bedroom Ranch homes, the most common home style. So what's my point?

The average sale price of the 97, 3-Bedroom Ranch style home sales in the South Colonie School District was $185,558 in 2016. Not too bad considering the same size and style home in the Troy School District only averaged $141,682 in 2016 (26, 3-Br Ranch sales). We see this comparison with the two tables below.

Figure 3.2: South Colonie School District <u>3-BR Ranch Homes</u> Sales: Final 2016

# of Home Sales	Avg Sale Price	Avg. Tax Amount
97	$185,558	$3,893

Courtesy of the Eastern NY Regional Multiple Listing Service from 1/1/2016 to 12/31/2016

Figure 3.3: Troy School District <u>3-BR Ranch Homes Sales</u>: Final 2016

# of Home Sales	Avg Sale Price	Avg. Tax Amount
26	$141,682	$5,098

Courtesy of the Eastern NY Regional Multiple Listing Service from 1/1/2016 to 12/31/2016

So the same exact home, with the same square footage, and number of bedrooms, can go for $40,000 more 20 minutes away across the Hudson River?

Notice how the tax amounts were higher for the Ranch style home sales in Troy, versus the average of tax amounts for South Colonie. The result, as we would expect, is higher sale prices for the sellers with lower taxes.

Remember, South Colonie Schools are currently ranked #4 overall in my rankings, with signs of threating to oust one of the other top three districts at the time of this writing. And yes, with low tax amounts and a desirable location, South Colonie has all the ingredients (key factors) of possessing high demand and attributes home buyers want.

Now, an added note about Figure 3.2 and Figure 3.3 on page 55, when comparing these home sales in two school districts. We can stop at the overall tax averages for all sales, and not segment by home style or square footage, but the idea here is to be proven **wrong** when you have a theory on what moves a home sale. Saying that higher tax amounts will drive down a home's sale price may seem like a matter of opinion, even if it sounds like common sense. Thus, looking at the housing statistics, and segmenting home sales using different attributes, all while comparing total tax amounts, helps back up a theory with solid statistics and data analysis. It now becomes fact and not an opinion.

So let's take it even further by using only one category as the focus of our in-depth analysis, and that is, **overall square footage** and compare the results to average sale price versus the overall tax amounts paid.

In 2016, 62 home sales in the South Colonie School District were advertised, and sold, as having less than 1,000 square feet. In fact, the average square footage of all 62 of these home sales came out to be just 863 square feet, on average. Not much space if you ask me.

Figure 3.4 on page 57, shows us how these 62 home sales, with under 1,000 square feet, still produced good results for their respective owners when it came to average sale price.

Figure 3.4: South Colonie School District Sales <u>Under 1,000 SqFt</u>. Final 2016

# of Homes	Avg Sq. Footage	Avg Sale Price	Avg. Tax Amount
62	863	$132,160	$2,694

Courtesy of the Eastern NY Regional Multiple Listing Service from 1/1/2016 to 12/31/2016

Not surprisingly, the average sale price was $132,160, with average tax amounts of $2,694 per year, for all sales. This is key information to discover a story through the data, that is telling us what home buyers desire and what is responsible for the sale of the homes. The average sale price here of $132,160 is quite prolific, considering these homes are no bigger than a college apartment. The lower tax totals that buyers pay means they are willing to spend more money on the sale price of the home and that's good news for sellers.

South Colonie School District is one of the best areas around for finding low taxes. But taxes are not a just a question for a home buyers monthly payment, some buyers are thinking about the possible long term repercussions when buying a home with high taxes, in relation to its resale value. While not enough home buyers are thinking about the future resale value of the home they are considering buying, I wish more would.

I recently worked with a couple on a home purchase, who took a step back and gave real thought about their future in a home they were considering buying. This home happened to have a total tax bill of around **$15,000** per year. When the kids were off to college, and maybe the home was paid off, they thought about having to pay that tax bill every year. They pictured themselves still paying over $1,000 per month for a home that would eventually have no mortgage. This fact alone was enough to make the decision that this home wasn't for them.

They ended up choosing a home in another school district that had significantly lower taxes and they were happy with their decision.

This is a good example of a real life situation where a potential home buyer backed away from a home purchase due to the future financial tax burden that the home had attached to it. Of course, they were also thinking about the resale implications to the next buyer that would have inherited such high property and school taxes.

I applaud the buyers for being smart and making a decision not to move forward with this home. Of course, they already were briefed on the whole tax issue, and when speaking to their mortgage rep, they already had a good idea of how important the taxes for the home are in relation to their monthly payment and affordability.

But there are times where tax amounts do not deter home buyers. In fact, it may not even be much of a thought to some. A good example of this can be seen within the Niskayuna zip code of 12309 and the Niskayuna School District. Take a look at Figure 3.5 for the final housing market stats in 2016, for the Niskayuna School District, and their total average tax amounts paid per home sale.

Figure 3.5: Niskayuna School District Sales: Final 2016

# of Home Sales	Avg Sale Price	Avg. Tax Amount
386	$263,479	$8,142

Courtesy of the Eastern NY Regional Multiple Listing Service from 1/1/2016 to 12/31/2016

In 2016, 386 homes saw a closing table in the Niskayuna School District. Based on the tax data the real estate agents entered into the MLS for each listing, the total average tax amounts paid per home, came out to be $8,142 per year. Ouch.

What's even more interesting is that the average home sale prices did not take much of a hit when you consider the final $263,479 average sale price. Over 60% of these 386 home sales saw their overall tax amounts to be at least $7,000. That means 230 or so, out of 386, all had total taxes quoted at this number, yet home buyers didn't waiver.

There is no doubt in my mind that if Niskayuna's overall tax averages came down to $4,000 per year compared to $8,000+ per year, we would see average sale prices there go well over $300,000. We know it's considered to be one of the more affluent areas in our region, whether simply due to opinion or not, it is the general consensus.

When we think about Niskayuna in general and relate it to Key Factor #1: Location, it really is a convenient spot for commuters, and even provides easy access to Saratoga County.

At the time of this writing, it currently ranks in the Top 10 for both zip code and school district. It is a high volume area, and demand does back up the supply. If you ask me, one of the main reasons Niskayuna isn't ranked higher is due to the high taxes as we just saw. But to people in a higher income bracket, it may be all relative. This is why a multitude of factors must be considered in the sale of your home.

In the case of Niskayuna, most home buyers can live with the high tax amounts. While sale prices are surely lower than they could be, they are still strong and demand still remains high in this area. Taxes should always go into factoring your asking price, but in the case of Niskayuna, taxes won't always be a reason why a home fails to sell. Unfortunately, there is nothing you can do about your taxes. Apart from pleading your case on grievance day, your taxes are here to stay and hopefully don't rise too dramatically during your span of ownership.

Come to think of it, all of the key factors we have discussed thus far are really out of your control. You won't be digging your house up, setting it on a flatbed and shipping it off to a new location. I guess it's possible, but the reality is that your homes location won't change.

The same can be said about your school district. Unless the school board and your local town does some sort of drastic merge where your school district suddenly changes, I think it's safe to say your school district is what it is.

These first three factors are out of your control. They cannot be changed and only understanding them, and accepting their effect on your home value, will help you be more comfortable, confident and successful with the sale of your home.

The good news is, the next two factors are under your complete control, and when understood, can be used to your advantage to discover hidden profits in your home sale. The next key factor is all on you. You have the control to change and manipulate your home in any way you see fit.

Yes, Key Factor #4 is Condition, if you haven't already guessed. No worries, this isn't the part where I tell you to get ready for a bunch of remodeling projects and spending all sorts of money. In fact, quite the opposite. But there are some nuances you should be aware of, and this is one of the biggest factors that will have the biggest impact on your sale.

Good news again is, you're in control.

KEY FACTOR #4: **CONDITION**

By Ryan Hoffman

Much is said about what return on investment can be had when making upgrades to your home. Whether it be a necessity or purely just for aesthetics, putting money into your existing home doesn't always mean big profits are going to come back to you in the sale.

In my opinion, aesthetic upgrades are more or less impossible to translate into more dollars at closing. While we can certainly see homes with full basements and garages sell for more money than those without, pinning a higher sale price on the basis of a recently remodeled bathroom or kitchen is just plain hard to do. How do you measure something that has so many variables?

So instead of thinking there is a concrete number that is needed to be found, let's just agree that a remodeled home will sell faster, and for more money, than one stuck in the 1970's. My point is simply stating that an exact ROI cannot be measured, regardless of the so-called experts who have tried to put these percentage returns on such upgrades. However, if you remodel a kitchen or bathroom inside your home, you will make your money back and possibly more, if you do it correctly. The secret is to upgrade for the next home buyer, not for yourself.

A small to average size kitchen can be remodeled with your local hardware stores stock counter tops and cabinetry for a few thousand dollars. Going with solid oak and granite on the other hand won't net you a return. This isn't a chapter on how to remodel your home, or what money to expect in return. Instead, this chapter is about the perception of home buyers, and why you need to cater to their view in order to have a quick sale with a high sale price.

It's not always about the bells and whistles. Home buyers, while sometimes mislead or misinformed in the real estate market, are, for the most part, aware of what they *should* be concerned with, even if they aren't sure *why* they should be concerned with it.

It's about presenting the home in a way that draws attention to space, and peace of mind. Homes need not be remodeled from top to bottom to sell for a good price, or to sell quickly. Cleanliness and lack of clutter can be enough to sell your home in a week when home buyers see the potential.

People are different. A potential fix or upgrade in your home may be a weekend project to some folks, and too much work for other folks. We aren't worried about catering to every need either. This is about presenting the home in a way that leads to fewer questions. The fewer questions home buyers ask, the better. The only questions we want to hear are: "How much are the taxes?" and "Do you have any offers yet?"

Once buyers begin asking a lot of questions related to the interior and exterior of the home, we begin to feel like we have to defend the condition of the home. This is especially true if the overall condition doesn't match up with our asking price.

Apart from the obvious, such as flooring, vanities, kitchens, baths and so on, what buyers are truly concerned with are the mechanical systems and the structure of the home overall, including the roof. Future issues and costs on a home are expected. But when it comes to pricing a home, we cannot expect a top neighborhood price if the roof is 30 years old, or the furnace is on its way out.

This is where price comes in. Let's for a second just assume your home is worth $250,000. If we put the home on the market for $100,000 what do you think would happen? There would probably be some skepticism due to the enormous bargain on the asking price, but I am sure there would be a line down the street of anxious home buyers looking to inherit some serious equity.

Your home would be sold in hours, not days.

On the flip side, let's price the same home at $500,000. What do you think would happen then? Most likely it would be quiet, and any showings you have would leave folks anxious to see what could possibly be going on inside this half-a-million dollar home.

And they better be impressed.

Drastic example, yes. But key to realize that price is the deciding factor here. All other factors lead up to your price. If I purchase your home with a 30 year old roof and 30 year old furnace, I am expecting to upgrade those items almost immediately after the closing. The idea is to be a happy home buyer who felt as if the price was reflective of the condition. Too many homeowners put an upgraded price on an outdated home.

Speed is an important factor if you ask me. Obviously as a potential home seller, I doubt your wish is for your home to sit on the market for half of a year, all while catering to showing after showing to home buyers who aren't even sure where or what they want to buy. Fast sale for the best price is the goal, and condition is something that you can control to get you there. Understanding the different levels of what good condition is can lead to a top sale price for your home.

The only way to convey what good condition looks like is to visit a home for sale in person, or sift through photos online and make your best judgements from real estate agents cell phone pics. Both are hard to do in a book format here, but there are a couple of other ways to conduct research and show examples of what good condition looks like by going inside the numbers.

One of those ways is to look at the average age of a home. Of course, a 15 year old Colonial home is expected to be more updated, closer to modern standards, and have just 15 years of wear on the roof and mechanical systems, compared to a home that is 50 years old.

Yes, older homes can be, and are, upgraded and remodeled all the time. Home owners of both remodeled homes and outdated "as-is" homes are still able to sell a home in a timely fashion for what they consider a good price. But the data tells us that older homes sell for less money than newer homes. We are just glad that statistical housing market data is there to back us up on what we already know to be true.

Let's take a look at some numbers and see the differences in average sale prices when compared to the age of the home. Then we can pick a few examples to go deeper. In 2016, 511 homes sold in the Clifton Park zip code. Many of which were between 20 and 50 years old.

Let's see how 2016 played out when comparing the age of the home to the average sale prices. On the following page, Figure 4.1 breaks down all home sales for 2016, in the 12065 zip code, and is sorted by the average age of the homes sold, from the youngest to the oldest. You can see Figure 4.1 on the next page.

Figure 4.1: 12065 Zip Code Sales by Age of Home : Final 2016

Age Range of home in years	# of Sales	Avg Sale Price
1-10	38	$365,553
11-20	87	$375,517
21-30	136	$244,849
31-40	97	$226,403
41-50	111	$246,244
50-100	37	$223,963
100+	5	$205,700

*Courtesy of the Eastern NY Regional Multiple Listing Service from 1/1/2016 to 12/31/2016

Again the data tells us a story. While not a perfect trend line overall, we see the differences in the average sale prices mostly decrease as the age of the home increases.

It's common sense to see what is happening here. New homes are selling for more money and the reason they are selling for more money is because they are more modernized. Everything from the roof and the mechanical systems, to the kitchens and baths are newer, or fairly so. **This exhibits good condition and good condition equals higher sale prices.**

But of course not everything is so cut and dry. We see 97 homes that sold for an average sale price of $226,403 were 31-40 years old. While 111 home sales averaged a final sale price of $246,244 were older homes averaging 41-50 years old. So what gives?

97 versus a 111 home sales in two different age brackets seems like a good matchup to determine how the older homes netted around $20,000 more. There is always at least a theory if not a solid answer. Lucky for you I've made it my business to find out why this is.

Sure enough I was able to see the discrepancy in the data. Of the 97 home sales that were 31 to 40 years old, a whopping 42 of them were Townhome sales. These Townhome sales skewed the average sale prices in this age bracket. After this discovery, I ran the data again, but this time, I eliminated Townhome styles from the research. Figure 4.2, shows the results from this new analysis.

Figure 4.2: All 12065 Zip Code Sale by Age: Final 2016

Age Range	# of Sales	Avg Sale Price
31-40	53	$270,682
41-50	104	$251,336

Courtesy of the Eastern NY Regional Multiple Listing Service from 1/1/2016 to 12/31/2016

With Townhome style home sales eliminated from the analysis, we see the younger homes had, in fact, sold for more money in 2016, as compared to the older homes in the 41 to 50 year range. It also gave us a good idea of how long ago the townhomes were built in Clifton Park.

Again, the idea is to always prove the factors wrong. While I don't expect every home sale to match perfectly with every measuring tool I use, we still want to discover why homes sell. If we had given up, without segmenting home styles in this example, we would have assumed that the theory of, an older home means less money, to be false.

There is no limit to segmenting real estate data. And with so many factors at play, well beyond my 5 Key Factors, there are a lot of moving parts to shuffle in an effort to get to the core of what makes a home sell fast, including how much money we can squeeze out of the sale. Stopping short of a few comps divided by three is like navigating a ship at sea without a compass. We need at least a general direction of where we are going and what to expect and using the statistical data and trends will help uncover a map that can get us right to the closing table.

Yes, as mentioned, you can always lower the price. But keeping the majority of your equity is the goal here. For some real estate agents, the best weapon seems to be just dropping the price over the course of months, or worse, years. When you are located in a high demand area, and you have plenty of equity, the ball is in your court. Don't just let an agent throw it out there to see what sticks. Go into the sale with a goal, and a strategy, and above all, information. Knowledge is power. (Another cliché that rings true but has lost its luster.)

When you possess something that others demand, you have the power. Even if you're not in one of the "Top 10" best real estate markets according to my rankings, you can still create leverage for your home sale, by using the 5 Key Factors in this book, as well as other pricing tools, to position yourself, and your home, as the ultimate value in the marketplace. Even a home owner in Hoosick Falls, an area troubled by a water crisis, can understand the market and the driving factors to then position the home in a way that creates demand and scarcity (fear of missing out).

If you're looking to test the market and see what bites, I get it. There are plenty of home owners that do this and they are not worried about time spent on the market or even the condition of their home. What they are really doing is just looking for feedback from the market. It's really not a bad strategy, which is why I often promote an online marketing campaign of the home for sellers that wish to "see what happens". I simply insist on getting feedback through photography and online advertising before locking into the MLS with an agent who could possibly ruin your bottom line with a track record of online price history.

Let's move on to other strategies we use to spot good home condition and see how it directly relates to the sale of your home. As mentioned earlier, sifting through photos on the MLS, or an online home site, is a good way to spot good condition. However, between bad real estate photography and lack of photos in some listings, the pictures we see of a home online can only take us so far.

Here we will discuss how we can look at the property description the real estate agents use and highlight some keywords that can be easily spotted, that tell us a whole lot about the home. When I do a market analysis, it helps to go beyond just the profile of the home. Segmenting the homes based on style, square footage, bedrooms, bathrooms and more, only gives us a detailed list of common homes. Now we have to look inside to see if we can figure out what made some homes sell faster than others especially when they are all similar homes.

Analyzing the Property Description

I'll do whatever it takes to pinpoint the exact reason a home sells fast and for a lot of money. Maybe it's a dumb thing to do considering it's obviously tough to measure such a thing. But you could reap the benefit if you follow the steps in this book and beyond to discover the hidden truth that gets home buyers to pay up. When searching all the homes that sold in Clifton Park in 2016, I came up with 506 home sales.

Well, actually, there were 511 home sales but 5 of the addresses were repeated, with two sales in a few months of each other. I'll explain why in a little bit. Anyway, of these 506 home sales, I ran a computer program that searches the property descriptions for each home that the agent typed in the MLS upon listing the home for sale. I searched for the word "remodeled" and it came back with 25 properties where the agent had used that word when describing the home. Figure 4.3 on the next page shows some of the findings from this research.

Figure 4.3: Search: "Remodeled" on all 2016 Clifton Park Home Sales: Top 5 Results

Home Details	Keyword detail	Days on Market
5 BR 2.5 BA Colonial	**Remodeled** bathroom.	0
4 BR 1.5 BA Colonial	**Remodeled** kitchen	0
4 BR 2 BA Split Level	**Remodeled** kitchen	0
4 BR 2 BA Raised Ranch	**Remodeled** kitchen	2
3 BR 1.5 BA Townhome	Completely **Remodeled**	4

We see the context of what the agent was referring to with the word "remodeled". Three were remodeled kitchens, one was a remodeled bathroom and one Townhome was completely remodeled. We also notice the days spent on the market before receiving an offer. All these homes sold instantly if not within the week.

So a remodeled bathroom was responsible for the sale of a home on the same day it was listed? Of course it helps in your home sale, but this was not the driving factor here. However, it did contribute to a quicker sale of these homes for sure. But we all know that a remodeled bathroom isn't the sole source for selling your home in basically one day.

When we see homes with zero days on market, that usually means the agent hosted an Open House on the same day they hit the "On" button for the MLS listing. Typically we see agents meet with home sellers and sign documents to list the home on a Monday, with plans on having an Open House the following Sunday. This way, they have time to get photos in order and announce the Open House to other agents and home buyers.

What's important to understand here is that the agent already knows the market is hot and hopes to get that price as competitive as possible. It's also worth mentioning that all five of the homes in this example sold for full price. If you ask me, selling for full price in a day means **losing money**. Think about Black Friday. Scores of people, literally trampling each other, some losing their lives, just to be the first person to grab a limited supply of 60-inch televisions that are marked as "50% off". When you get to the cash register on Black Friday, there is no further haggling. The price is a deal to begin with and you're happy to pay it.

Analyzing the lot size and yard layout.

When I talk about "Condition" as Key Factor #4, I should have mentioned that the yard, lot layout, and other subtle details are always included in the conversation. Obviously you cannot fix a yard that drops off into a ravine, or is on the smaller side, but knowing what you have, and that it matters, means you are close to understanding your home and what it has going for it.

I listed a home just this past year that was just seven years old. However, the yard was small, and the layout of the yard was not ideal for kids or pets to run around in. I've attached a couple examples of what that feedback looked like, from agents who had shown this listing.

Figure 4.4 shows a couple of feedback examples from this listing. Please disregard the clarity of these screen shots. I had to copy them off of the computer screen as they are not official photos. Nevertheless, it is a glimpse into what real feedback looks like on a home listed right here in our area.

Figure 4.4: Feedback examples from agents who showed a home I had listed. Note the comments about the yard.

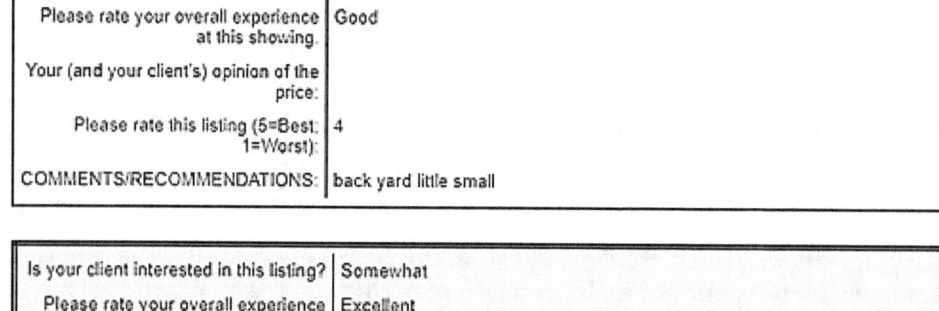

The feedback indicated what I had already knew. Homes in the immediate area were selling much faster and for around the same price as we were asking. When I researched these sales I saw that all of them had a nice, square, flat back yard, which is as good as it gets for home buyers with children and pets.

But, let me get back on track with using keywords to understand how a home can be positioned in the market to sell fast and for the most money. I know I said that the five home sales in Figure 4.3 on page 70, all sold for full price and probably all lost money. I still believe that. These homes could still have sold within 30 days for an extra $5,000, $10,000, even $20,000 dollars.

It may sound stupid to say, but $10,000 to $20,000 is not that much money in the grand scheme of real estate. Price reductions usually happen in five-figure increments. Dropping the price $10,000 isn't out of this world, in fact, it's common, even when it's still not enough to spark an offer. To a home buyer, especially one who is aware, realize that an extra $10,000, stretched out over 30 years, isn't increasing their monthly payment too drastically. In most cases, it wouldn't even exceed $50 extra per month.

For the Colonial homes that sold for $257,000 (full price), on the same day it hit the MLS, you think they couldn't have gotten more money out of a home sale? How hard would it be to take a $257,000 home and price it at $267,000? Or $275,000? It wouldn't. And if you ask me, I would have put it on for $279,000. If you don't want an extra $20,000 from your home sale, I am sure there are people out there that would take it off your hands for you.

Regardless, these homes had other things going for them besides possibly being underpriced. Here are some other words and phrases I found to be important features that helped the home be more marketable.

Newer roof, new gas fireplace, new septic tank, new vinyl siding, refinished hardwoods, new carpet, new furnace (2010), Central A/C replaced (2012), mature trees, privacy fence, dead end street, new electric.

We are adding up all the parts to equal the whole picture. Chances are you have had to replace some things since you have owned your home. The idea is to ease the buyers mind by helping them realize they won't have to spend money on repairs for some time. Even just one upgrade in the grand scheme of things, can help you. You could have kitchen countertops, carpeting and vanities from the 1990's, but the roof was just replaced and the furnace is new. This is as good as anything, especially in top demand areas. As long as your home is free of clutter, clean and presentable, home buyers will reward you in the end.

If you often dream about quitting your job and flipping homes for a living, like they do on TV, then you're going to like this next section. We are going to stay in Clifton Park and look at how we spotted the homes that investors had bought, and flipped, and also see what price a fully remodeled home can fetch inside, what is usually, our areas #1 real estate market.

Flipping houses in the #1 market

OK, so you received this book on how to price your home to sell for the most money, not because you wanted to flip houses. So what is the point of this next section? The idea here is to drive home the point that condition is a key factor which is responsible for the sale of your home. The condition of the home, including its lot size and layout, all lead to your asking price in conjunction with the other key factors in this book. Since the homes in this next section are completely remodeled, we know that the final sales prices here, reflect the great condition of these homes, after being remodeled.

After Key Factor #5 is covered in the next chapter, I will be sharing with you 5 Case Studies of my own listings that show which Key Factor, or combination of Key Factors, were responsible for the sale. It will be a great opportunity for you to see some of my own sales that I can share with you that you can search online to see more details on these homes for yourself.

But in the meantime, let's check out three home sales that I recognized as "flips" in the list of all Clifton Park (12065 Zip Code) sales in 2016. The reason these sales jumped out at me was simple, they were repeated in the list of home sales for the entire year. I was able to spot that these home sales with the same address, had sold twice within just a few months and for much higher prices than the first sale. These were no-doubt homes that were flipped for profit.

I am going to call these three sales #1, #2 and #3. Pertaining to the disclosure in the beginning of this book, I will hold back on revealing the physical addresses of these properties, but explain the details of what these homes had going for them, what they didn't have, and to see if any money was lost in either of the sales. We will also look into why one of these homes failed to sell for almost 90 days even though it was remodeled.

Flip #1

Here is what I spotted in the MLS for Flip #1 in Clifton Park in Figure 4.5:

Figure 4.5: Sale dates and prices of Flip #1 in Clifton Park

Sale Date	Sale Price	Days on Market
3/3/16	$150,000	1
6/30/16	$251,750	6

1st Sale: March 3rd, 2016

This home was a 4 bedroom, 1.5 bathroom, Split-Level home, with 1,976 square feet and an approximate age of 49 years old. The home was vacant, and with plenty of photos available, I could see the work that needed to be done.

There were some hardwood floors in the living room when you walked in, but otherwise there was wall-to-wall carpeting throughout the home that looked like it was from the 1970's or 1980's. There was even carpeting in the kitchen if that helps put things into perspective. There was no visual drywall in the photos, it consisted of wood paneling throughout the entire home, as well as wallpaper covering the walls of the other rooms in the house. (I assume there was drywall beneath the wallpaper and faux wood paneling)

The heating system looked to be somewhat upgraded, at least showing new copper piping in the photos. The water heater looked like a recent upgrade as well. There was no property disclosure document in the MLS listing to indicate the age or condition of any other important features, and the home sold after just one day on the market for $150,000. One interesting note was that the home was sold as a 3 bedroom home, but once remodeled and put back on the market, it was advertised as a 4 bedroom home. The tax record indicated it was labeled as a 3 bedroom home.

2nd Sale: June 30th, 2016

The agent's remarks about the home indicated that all the windows had been replaced but the roof was not. Based on a picture online, the roof seemed like the shingles were in good shape. The before and after photos on this one were truly astounding, I will admit. They really left no stone unturned here with the work that was put into it.

It looked like they caught a break with not having to do the heating system or the roof. Everything else was just aesthetically upgraded. The hardwood floors were stripped, sanded and sealed. Brand new kitchen from the floor to the backsplash, counter tops and appliances. New carpeting in certain areas like the sun room, and freshly painted walls. There were also a few shrubs removed outside for curb appeal. Certainly an extensive job that looks like it was knocked out by a big crew. They turned it around in just over three months for a gross profit of $100,000. We don't know what they spent to fix of course, but I am sure a nice profit was made.

So what do we see? Again, don't get discouraged and think I am implying that you have to renovate your entire home. In fact, I will show you case studies near the end of this book that prove you can sell fast, and for the most money, without doing a thing but vacuuming. People flip homes for a reason, and that reason isn't just the fact that it can be profitable, it's more about the fact that some home buyers really don't want to do a lot of work to a home they buy, and that is why a home in great condition can sell fast and for top dollar.

Overall, the original home seller lost some money here in my opinion. People sell their home for many reasons, and this particular sale looked like it could have been an estate sale, and was left to heirs to sell after a loved one passed. With that possibly being the case, you'd be surprised to find that some folks just need to get rid of the home and aren't concerned about squeezing every dime out of the sale.

Either way, the home sold for $150,000 but was asking $145,000. They received $5,000 **over** asking price in 1 day, which tells me they could have sold it for probably $160,000, easily. Especially with 1,976 square feet. You would think $10,000 would mean a lot to people, but some home sale scenarios carry different reasons and motivations behind the sale, or of course the agent priced it incorrectly.

As far as the investors were concerned, they sold the home in 6 days for basically $100,000 gross profit. They were asking $259,900 and ended up with around 96.5% of their asking price. Considering that the Clifton Park average in 2017 is around 98%, at the time of this writing, I think at best, they could have gotten another $2,500 out of this 2nd sale, and I am sure there were multiple offers. But a $100,000 gross profit is good, and a quick sale for the most profit was evident. Now let's take a look at Flip #2 on the next page.

Flip #2

Figure 4.6: Sale dates and prices of a Flip #2 in Clifton Park

Sale Date	Sale Price	Days on Market
5/17/16	$190,000	5
9/29/16	$242,500	22

1st Sale: May 5th, 2016

This home was a 3 bedroom, 2 bathroom Contemporary home with 1,764 square feet. Picture a Ranch style home that gets hitched up with a Cape Cod style home. It was advertised as a 38 year old home, and luckily, had plenty of photos on the listing to take a further look. Ironically, the agent indicated that the "price reflects the condition", go figure, but this home had a pretty unique layout and looked like a cool place.

The home was located on a corner lot, and had some wooden privacy fence in the back yard. While it looked like it needed some attention, overall it was a good lot that would attract a buyer with children or pets. It was also located across the street from the park that was designated for the particular housing development it was located in.

This Contemporary home did give the feel of an open floor plan. But really it was the oversized living room and master bedroom with two walk in closets that chewed up much of the square footage. The bedrooms and bathrooms were of average size and the kitchen was as well. But the main thing about this home was the fact that it already had updated countertops and cabinetry, so those two items were taken care of, plus some of the windows were already upgraded. This helped save the investor some cash. The big bonus was the property disclosure sheet indicated the roof was only 12 years old, thus the investor need not worry about this expense either. The home sold for $190,000 in just 5 days.

2nd Sale: September 29th, 2016

The home was upgraded with new flooring throughout. It was a combination of new carpeting and laminate wood flooring. Some windows were upgraded and the entire home was painted. This was 70% of it right off the bat.

There were a decent amount of features that remained unchanged that I mentioned from the first sale of this home. Those being the countertops, cabinets, shower, tub surround and shower doors. Other items such as bathroom vanity and sink, toilets, closet doors and interior doors were changed. Also outside, there was a cleanup done of the landscaping and some crushed stone laid down around the walkway. The home was also professionally staged, meaning it was furnished throughout. A technique that myself, other agents, and of course you, could utilize if you want to get the most money for your home. Granted, it's much easier to stage an investment property than it is to stage a home you've lived in for 25 years.

All in all, this was a lighter workload for this investor, with a few big items taken care of before they had purchased it. I was glad to see the owner originally fetched $190,000 in the first sale, for a home that had some things going for it, but still knew where they stood within the market. They did list the home at $188,800, which means it was bid up, most likely, by multiple bidders. Right off the bat I say this home should have been $199,000 with a possible sale at full price, if not, $195,000. I mean…its only $5,000 right?....*sheesh*

It took 22 days on the market for the second sale of this home. Do you think they could have gotten more? I actually love their pricing strategy here. To get this sale done within 30 days is the ultimate goal.

I don't like to see a home sell in a day as you know money was left behind. They started at $259,900, and after 20 days, they dropped the price by just $1,000 to $258,900 and that was enough to get an offer three days thereafter. While they didn't get a full price offer, their asking price was good enough to entice an offer.

This pricing schedule was hit perfectly, and it leaves behind a feeling that there was no money left behind. There is no thought of "what could have been" like there could be in most home sales, when it comes to netting the most cash that is. This flip ended up with just over $50,000 in gross profit. Not a bad income for just one-third of the year. Of course this isn't what the investor netted in the end, but the condition of this home from the beginning made this flip a sort of "paint by numbers", ready for just a few touches that took less work and less money to get done.

So let's take a look at Flip #3. Figure 4.7 shows us the two separate sales dates and respective sale prices for this property.

Flip #3

Figure 4.7: Sale dates and prices of Flip #3 in Clifton Park

Sale Date	Sale Price	Days on Market
3/14/16	$201,000	23
9/16/16	$307,500	77

1st Sale: March 14th, 2016

This home was interesting to look at because it was only 21 years old. This is still a fairly new home, considering the broad spectrum of homes in our region, as well as how old some areas date back. It was a 4 bedroom and 2.5 bathroom Colonial home. It was marketed at 1,816 square feet, with a full basement which was finished. It's also important to note that the home was bank owned and being sold at auction. Bottom line profit concern for the bank here is irrelevant, so I won't talk about that too much.

The home looks massive in the photos due the attached 2 car garage with a bonus room over it. It had vinyl siding, and you quickly realize that everything about the home is just 21 years old. That means the roof itself could possibly have 15 or more years of life left on it. The windows were very nice 6 panel vinyl windows, so that cost was avoided. It also had a nice flat yard in the front and in the back, with some trees lining the back yard for privacy.

It was in dire need of a power wash, and there really was no curb appeal to speak of. Once I saw the inside photos, I could tell right away that everything was probably original. Everything looked like builder grade for the time period of when it was built. Vinyl flooring, laminate countertops, wall paper and wood paneling, plus all the vanities, tub surround and accessories were consistent with a home built in the 1990's.

2nd Sale: September 16th, 2016

The home stood out even more than it had in the first sale when looking at the photos. The front of the house actually had a wraparound porch to the right of it that was not visible before. Definitely a cool bonus and a result from having professional landscapers do the job, which made the home look bigger than before.

The kitchen was completely gutted and more counter space was added compared to what was originally there. They had everything redone, from tile floor in the kitchen, new cabinets, new granite countertops, and all new stainless steel appliances. It looked sharp. The whole house had new flooring throughout with a combination of tile, carpet, and hardwood flooring, some real and some laminate. Also new paint, of course, and some interior doors with updated hardware. It looked like they went ahead and put a new roof on this home as well. The bathrooms were remodeled but some things were able to remain, such as the toilets and a jetted tub in the master bath. All in all the main cost here looked to be the roof and the kitchen when it came to materials and labor. Flooring was a decent chunk of money as well. Nothing else seemed to indicate other major costs had taken place. The total gross profit here was $106,000. That is a nice profit, but it did take 77 days to sell, plus the two months it took to remodel. Still, at this gross profit, the 77 days were worth it to this investor.

Here we see a home that is now virtually maintenance free for the first few years of owing it, with **condition** being the main reason why. But why didn't we see this home sell is just a matter of days after the flip? The answer is in their price strategy.

The investors were a bit over zealous with this one. They put the home on the market for $350,000. That's $43,000 over where they ended up selling it. It turns out that the listing agent was also involved with the flip, so he had a vested interest. And this is our telling point here, the agent being involved with this investment, if not just financially but also possibly physically. He saw his hard work and money turn this home into something really nice, right before his eyes.

With this emotional attachment, the investors in this case, saw the home as being worth more than it really was, seemingly without studying the current Clifton Park market. They learned the hard way about getting too excited about big profits. To an investor, time is truly money, and it should be for you as well. Apart from the cost to remodel, each day and each month the home is for sale, and not selling, owners are paying taxes, utilities, catering showings to no avail, and wondering how much longer they should go before pulling the plug. Figure 4.8 on the next page shows us the price schedule for Flip #3.

Figure 4.8: MLS property history for Flip #3

Date	Action	Price
6/02/2016	Listed for Sale	$350,000
6/07/2016	Price Drop	$343,500
6/24/2016	Price Drop	$330,000
7/06/2016	Price Drop	$325,000
8/04/2016	Withdrawn	$325,000
8/11/2016	Pending	$325,000
9/30/2016	Sold	$307,500

Priced at $350,000, new to the market at the beginning of June 2016. After just 10 days, the price came down just $6,500 to $343,500. The agent probably got a bulk of new showings based on the location and the condition, but went without offers, so he dropped it just a little. After two more weeks, he made a big jump, down to $330,000. This was at the 30th day on the market.

So the home is remodeled, practically brand new, 30 days on, and not sold. What gives? It's just simply a matter of price. In this case, lack of market research, and experience, leads to over pricing.

Two weeks later, another $5,000 drop. Down to $325,000. Then the agent stops. He feels he has to be close. In just over 1 month he has come down $25,000 and still no offers. $325,000 has to get it done at this point right? For 30 more days they wait, this time, with no price drops. Then suddenly, something unexpected happened, the home was withdrawn from the market on August 4th.

At $325,000, now at the beginning of August, this home just saw the bulk of its home buying season come and go with nothing more than a $25,000 drop and a lot of anxiety mounting. But alas, there is action. Just one week after the home was withdrawn, it's suddenly under contract? And 45 days later, was published as sold for $307,500.

So what happened? I can take a guess, and I bet I'd be pretty accurate. Once the home was pulled off the market, scarcity set in. Interested home buyers, that may had even seen the home already, liked the home a lot, but were literally frozen by the price. Buyers and their agents aren't always willing to come in with an offer way below your asking price. In this case the agent may have pulled the home off the market, then received a phone call from an buyer's agent and had a conversation that went something like this:

"Hey look, my folks love the home, but were hesitant to offer because of the price. Are you guys able to work with us on this price a bit?"

I could be wrong, but this is usually how it has gone in my experience. It would explain why the home would actually receive an offer after it was pulled from the market, and that offer ended up being another **$17,500** off their final asking price of $325,000. This is also assuming they negotiated and ended up at $307,500. The buyer could have offered $300,000 and knew these investors were sweating. In the end the home sold, and the gross profit was there. That's all that matters. I'm sure these investors were still happy with $100K+ gross profit, I know I would be.

The underlying message on Key Factor #4, **Condition**, is that, perception is always reality. And the perception of your homes condition can certainly be in your control. I will show you in my case studies that a remodeled home is not necessary in order to sell fast or for the most money. But using remodeled homes, in which some are flipped by investors, helps to drive home the fact that condition is a huge factor that needs to weighed heavily when determining the asking price.

You don't need to worry about what your home does or doesn't have right now, or more importantly, what it actually needs. All you need to realize is we must weigh all features and benefits of the homes interior, and exterior, to come to a more realistic price that will get the most money out of the home sale.

Thinking again about this more recent flip, **Flip #3**, they ended up selling for $307,500 after over pricing the home drastically. If they started at the $325,000 or even $319,000, there is probably a good chance they would have gotten over $310,000 for the home instead of $307,500. We also saw the listing agent was part of the investment here, and that put emotional attachment into the home, just as you probably have with your own home. As hard as it is, you must look at your home from an outsider's perspective as someone who's never been in it.

You've made it this far, and frankly, I am flattered. I thank you for taking the time to read this book in an effort to help yourself be prepared to defend your equity when it comes time to list your home for sale.

That just leaves one key factor left and we will have covered The 5 Keys Factors to selling your home in the Capital Region? Are you ready? There is no better time than now. Speaking of timing...

DEFEND YOUR EQUITY

KEY FACTOR #5: **TIMING**

By Ryan Hoffman

Everything in life really comes down to timing. The sale of your home is no different. Striking while the iron is hot can ensure that your home sale is smooth, stress free, and most importantly, fast.

Of course getting the most money for your home is the ultimate goal. We have seen some examples where homes are selling on the same day its listed, while others sell within just one week. But selling too quickly can mean leaving money on the table in some cases.

I believe every home should sell within 90 days, tops. There is no need to sit on the market for 6 to 12 months, not sell, and then just drop the price over and over again. This is where home sellers become frustrated and confused. Feeling as if your home will never sell begets the question: Why?

Most home owners who fail to sell are disgruntled with their agent, and sometimes it is justified. Most agents lack a pricing strategy to begin with, let alone an ongoing line of communication during the process.

As I have touched on in this book, most agents don't have a plan of action for your home sale. They just operate on price reductions and the biggest obstacle to overcome is simply winning your business. I mean if I took my pricing strategy and told you, after in-depth research and irrefutable evidence, that your home is worth $250,000 you may be happy. But if another agent says it's worth $275,000 with no pricing strategy, more often than not, home sellers will go with the agent who tells them a higher price. This is a fatal mistake you must avoid.

When real estate agents are competing for a listing, where the seller is interviewing multiple agents, they like to over quote your home value in an effort to win the business. Of course, when there are no other agents gunning for the listing, the sole listing agent is more comfortable pricing the home accurately due to the lack of competing agents vying for the business.

But once you sign on the dotted line for your 6 to 12 month agreement, you're locked in. Most home sellers don't realize how stuck they are when they list their home for sale. Agents literally have you cornered. Even the use of your attorney can be fruitless if you try to cancel the listing agreement. The standard MLS agreements that we use in our area are templates. It is simply a fill-in-the-blank, two page contract, that was written by New York State attorneys. Did you know that an MLS listing agreement actually states that you're obligated to pay a commission to your agent if an offer is made on your home but not accepted?

The verbiage in the listing agreement states that your agent's job is to bring you an offer. That's it. It doesn't say it has to be accepted. And if you don't accept an offer, legally, your agent is still entitled to be paid, and some agents have received a commission check when suing a home owner who did not accept one of the many offers that came forward during the listing in which the seller declined. So what does this have to do with timing? Everything.

Being locked into an agreement, being misled on price, and languishing on the internet (MLS), where home buyers begin to ask **"What's wrong with that house, it's been on the market awhile?"** can absolutely ruin your timing and your price. While homes do sell year round in our area, it's no surprise or secret that, when looking at the housing market data, homes listed for sale, and homes that are sold, dip drastically in the Fall and Winter months.

Between the local schools being back in session, the change of the seasons, holidays and of course, the cold, brutal winters we face in Upstate New York, listing your home for sale in November, or January, can sometimes mean waiting a while for a sale.

Let's take a look at the housing market statistics on a month to month basis, using Saratoga County, to see the differences in homes listed and homes sold based on the time of year. Figure 5.1 on the next page, shows a table of all homes listed and sold in Saratoga County for the calendar year of 2016. You will notice how the number of homes listed for sale rise during the Spring and Summer months, and decreases into the Fall and Winter months.

Figure 5.1: Saratoga County Homes Listed and Sold: All 2016

Month	Listed	Sold
January	226	162
February	206	146
March	347	169
April	356	182
May	410	230
June	404	270
July	365	287
August	322	292
September	291	246
October	246	232
November	198	188
December	126	213

Courtesy of the Eastern NY Regional Multiple Listing Service from 1/1/2016 to 12/31/2016

Notice how May and June posted the most listing for the year. And December of course, showed only 126 homes listed in all of Saratoga county. Of course, this shouldn't be shocking to you.

When Spring starts to get closer, folks are already planning on selling their home. They are most likely doing small projects around the house, or anything that they think will get their home ready to sell and be more desirable to a home buyer.

While March and April marks the beginning of "listing season", many home buyers are not ready until the month of May. Some plan on using their tax returns to use towards the closing costs. While not all home buyers rely on tax season to buy a home, most first-time home buyers do. Plus home buyers know that there will be more homes to choose from come the Spring and early Summer months, as compared to the end of Winter. **This is where home sellers can capitalize.**

It's understandable however, to realize that not all home sellers have a choice when they choose to list their home, regardless of the time of year. For the 126 home sellers that hit the market in December 2016 in Saratoga County in Figure 5.1, I have to think that most of them knew the timing for selling a home wasn't all that great. Of course real estate agents are happy to oblige.

People sell a home for a lot of different reasons, and yes, home buyers are always in the market to buy. Homes do receive contracts 52 weeks a year, and home buyers, like sellers, cannot always wait to make a move. If you have the luxury of waiting, my suggestion would always be to list your home on May 1st. Yes, March heats up, and April as well, but May seems to be the sweet spot for giving you the best advantage when it comes to selling your home.

Let's take an in-depth look at some real life sales in Clifton Park where timing made a difference and also some examples of where home owners were able to use the other four key factors to sell their home fast in the dead of winter. I am going to show you some examples of home sales that are seemingly identical, but have very different outcomes.

I am going to use some home sales in the Clifton Park zip code of 12065. I am going to zone in on 4 bedroom, 2.5 bath Colonial homes **ONLY.** This is going to give us a lot of specific examples. Plus, I will keep the square footage in range as well, so we can get as close as possible to comparing these similar homes.

Again due to the MLS rules and regulations, I am going to leave the physical addresses out of these examples. However, these are real sales that have occurred between 2016 and 2017 in Clifton Park. While home sale data is public record, for precautionary reasons, I will omit the addresses and just focus on the details.

Let's use a range from September 2016 to June of 2017. This way we can see the differences between the homes listed in the Fall and Winter, versus the homes listed in the Spring and early Summer, to see how timing played a role in the sale of the home.

The next page depicts the home sales I found, to compare the outcomes based on their timing when hitting the market. I was able to narrow down the criteria to four home sales. Here is the criteria that I have set up for this example:

- 4 Bedroom
- 2.5 Bathroom
- Colonial style
- 2 car garage
- Full, finished basement.
- 2400-2600 square feet.

Remember, we are dealing with homes in Clifton Park. It's safe to say we are narrowed in pretty good. So how do these sales shake out? Let's have a look at Figure 5.2 on the next page, showing us just four home sales based on all of this criteria.

Figure 5.2: Four Colonial home sales in 12065 (Clifton Park)

Home Sale	Listing Month	Sale Price	Days on Market
Sale #1	December	$320,000	85
Sale #2	March	$321,000	13
Sale #3	April	$330,500	5
Sale #4	May	$325,000	7

It's not a coincidence that the days on market is decreasing as the warmer weather hits. I've highlighted Sale #1 to show you how the home still sold for a similar price as all the other three homes but stayed on the market for 3 months. They ended up closing in May, so what would have happened if they just listed it then instead of December? This is where timing can affect your price.

What I didn't show you in the table above was the asking price of these homes in comparison to the sale price. Remember, these homes are practically identical. With just a couple hundred square feet of difference. We aren't breaking down the condition, just the details of size, similar attributes and location. So what's the difference between listing a home in December, waiting 90 days to sell for a similar price than all the other homes that list in the Spring? Have a look at Figure 5.3 on the next page.

Figure 5.3: Four Colonial home sales, difference in List Price vs. Sale Price

Home Sale	List Price	Sale Price	Profit vs Asking Price
Sale #1	$334,900	$320,000	-$14,900
Sale #2	$314,900	$321,000	+$6,000
Sale #3	$329,900	$330,500	+$600
Sale #4	$319,000	$325,000	+$6,000

What did all of these sales have in common? Three of the four sold for over asking price, and the reason was the timing.

By the time home buyers were out looking for a home in the Spring, they perceived Sale #1 as a "problem" home. When a home sits on the market for a long period of time home buyers recognize this. Thus, the home sold for almost $15,000 off the original asking price that was set in December.

The other three sales all sold in just 1-2 weeks, and, they all sold for over the asking price. Since it was Spring, and most of the home buyers were out looking, competition had increased, and homes were being bid up. But for Sale #1, it was perceived as a home that has been on the market for a while, and it created an opportunity for a home buyer to get it for less.

Sale #1 settled at $320,000, which means the buyer may have offered $310,000. After a brief negotiation, I assume, they settled at $320,000. When we fast forward to the Spring, we see the three other practically identical homes, selling for over asking price. They were new to the market in the Spring, when more buyers are out looking. The sellers for sales #2, #3 and #4 had the upper hand in the transaction. They offered their home up for sale at a time when home buyer demand would be at its peak. Timing was a key factor.

Sale #1, had bad timing. Even if this particular owner had to list the home based on some personal reasons, they still didn't see a closing until May anyway. So do you think they could have made more money off of the sale? Absolutely.

While they were the highest priced home in the four comparisons, they actually sold for the least amount of money. Even home sale #3 listed for $329,900 and still received an amount over asking price. If Sale #1 listed their home in May, for $320,000 instead of $334,900, there was a very good chance they could have seen their home fought over and bid up to $325,000.

This seller left money behind due to bad timing when listing their home in December. For three months, with low buying demand during the Winter, their price became ruined and home buyers perceived this home as an opportunity to get some money off its asking price. Of course we know there is nothing "wrong" with the home, but home buyers see it differently.

However, it's not always an issue of just being overpriced. While $334,900 may have been too high of an asking price even if they went with that in May, it still comes down to timing the sale based on the demand that is in the market. This book started out with talking about Supply and Demand, and home buyer demand heats up in the early Spring, and peaks in the Summer. Line your home sale up with this fact, and you create a whole lot of leverage to get you the most money.

High demand always increases the price on a product. No matter what industry. Sale #1 may not have been overpriced after all. Maybe they could have listed it at $334,900 in May and gotten full price, or even $330,000. It would have been very possible due to buyer competition and home buyers concern of missing out. This always alters the perception in the market and Clifton Park is usually the #1 in-demand zip code in our region. Also, Colonial style home sales in Clifton Park are the most common, most sought after, and fetch the highest sale price. Line all this up with a listing date of May 1st, and you're guaranteed to make the most money possible.

There are thousands of examples like this, all over the Capital Region. And as stated, not all home sellers have a choice. Maybe there was a job transfer and you have to sell now? Or maybe you're tired with the Northeast winter weather? (more likely) But regardless of personal needs, timing is key. Hoping for the best when listing your home in the winter won't always equate to a sale.

But not all is lost. What about those December listings that are under contract in just a few days? Well, besides being underpriced, do you think we can find out how some fast winter home sales had used their overall position to guarantee a sale? I have one in mind.

How did a home, that listed two days after Christmas, sell in a matter of one week? For this next example, the answer is in the details.

Without revealing someone's physical address, I will tell you that this home is located in Crescent Estates South in Clifton Park. It was found using the criteria from the last example. This was a 4 bedroom, 2.5 bathroom Colonial home with a full, finished basement and a two car garage.

Colonial home sales in Clifton Park range from the low-to mid $200,000's, all the way up to $400,000+ range. For this particular example, the home settled at $286,000. So what were the driving factors that had this home under contract is just 6 days right after Christmas?

The answer in this case, was condition and, ultimately, price. The caveat to this example was this home was already on the market before. They actually listed the home in October and for 82 days nothing happened. The starting price was $309,000 when the home was listed in October. When they re-listed the home again, in December, they dropped the asking price to $299,000 and accepted an offer just six days thereafter which closed at $286,000.

The one thing this home had going for it, besides its desirable location, was its immaculate condition. Not only was it decorated for the minimalist in mind (clutter free), there was also a lot of upgrades that included a new kitchen remodel, new bath remodel, new furnace, central air unit and more. The photos were done professionally and shot before the leaves fell. So even though the home was on the market in the Fall and early Winter, the photos were showing a nice sunny day that looked more like a Summer afternoon.

The point to this second example is to show you that on the surface, things aren't always what they seem. As soon as you think the theory of timing is not always in play, we dive deeper and see that, in this example, it most certainly was. The home was listed twice, the second time being the "fast sale". This is why in-depth research and knowledge is so beneficial for home sellers to know.

If you couldn't tell by now, this isn't a surefire example of how to sell your home just six days after Christmas. Its deceiving when we realize that the home was actually on the market prior for 80+ days, and then relisted as a "new listing". The fact here is, the timing wasn't great at all. Listing the home in October originally, for over $300,000, was detrimental to the home sellers bottom line. They re-listed the home with a price drop and the home sold quickly. In my opinion, the seller could have waited until May to list the home for sale at $299,000 and probably seen it get bid up to $310,000. Based on the photos, description of upgrades and location, this home could have sold for the price the seller wanted, if only they used timing in their favor.

Timing is always important when selling your home. If you insist on listing your home in the later months of the year, be prepared to wait some time before an interested buyer comes around. Unfortunately, too many home sellers lose patience. Then it becomes just a price game. While this book is about the 5 Key Factors that lead to your asking price, we don't always want to rely on price reductions just to get a sale. Heck, dropping the price is easy.

So that's it right? The 5 Key Factors that all lead to your asking price? Admittedly, there is much more to pricing your home. In fact, I have a 21-Point Checklist that needs to be factored in once we get past the 5 Key Factors. I had already touched on some aspects included in this checklist. But the point is, weighing all pros and cons inside and outside your home, and comparing them to other home sales that have similar attributes, is important.

There is a difference in sale prices for homes that have a 2-car garage compared to a 1-car garage. And there is an even bigger difference between home sale prices for homes with a 2-car garage and a home that doesn't have a garage at all. Same goes for basements. Full basement or a slab? Is the Full basement finished?, even better. There are many features to a home that can be measured with data analytics, while some features simply cannot be measured at all, but instead are used as wild cards to help determine the asking price.

My game is using a pricing strategy to squeeze, literally, every penny out of your equity when selling, which could be upwards of $100,000, depending on where your home is located and how long you've been there. Ask any baby-boomer home owner in Clifton Park what they purchased their home for 30 years ago, compared to today's average sale prices, and you'd see that $100,000 in equity isn't farfetched.

For those that have such equity, an extra $5,000 or $10,000 left behind, may be just a drop in the bucket, but as I have said before in this book, if you aren't needing that extra cash, there is a long line of folks who could use it.

So let's get to some real life examples to see these 5 Key Factors really in play. This time, I get to use the physical address of these home sales, since I was the agent who helped the home seller get the best price for their home.

I will present to you five case studies, of five home sales that I represented over the past couple of years. Each home is located in different areas of our region, and are very different from one another. I will show you the 5 Key Factors that were at play with each home sale, including how the pricing of the home ultimately led to an offer.

You will also hear about different situations and challenges that were faced apart from pricing the home correctly and getting it sold. After you read these case studies, you'll be able to see all of the 5 Key Factors represented in some form or another, and also learn how to avoid some common, and some not so uncommon, pitfalls when it comes to selling your own home.

DEFEND YOUR EQUITY

CASE STUDY #1

By Ryan Hoffman

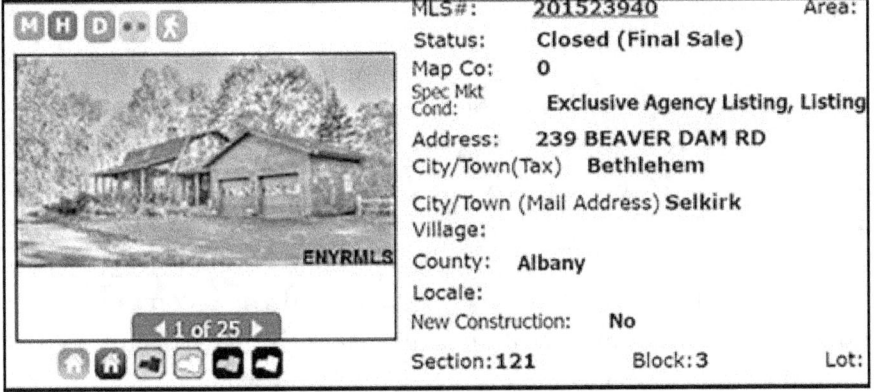

Address: 239 Beaver Dam Rd. Selkirk, NY

Zip Code: 12158

Zip Code Rank: 48th out of 70

School District: Ravena-Coeymans

School District Rank: 25th out of 49

THE DETAILS

239 Beaver Dam Road, is a 3 bedroom and 1.5 bathroom, Log style home. It had 1,824 square feet and a full, unfinished basement. The home boasted a great lot at 4.75 acres, a very beautiful setting, however, it did border up to the local CSX train tracks. Trains were close to the rear of the lot, and sometimes would sit there overnight. The utilities (water and sewer) were public, which was a bonus. Other features worth mentioning are hardwood flooring, formal dining room, wood fireplace with field stone chimney, and also an in-ground pool in the back yard.

Let's breakdown the story of how this home lined up with the 5 Key Factors, and ultimately, how we got this home sold.

LOCATION

239 Beaver Dam Road was not a home located in a high demand area. The Selkirk, NY zip code of 12158 finished as the 48th best real estate market in 2016, based out of the 70 zip codes I rank. This tells us where we stand within the market.

From downtown Albany, it really isn't a bad drive to commute when you think about this homes location. This would also have been a good location for anyone who worked south of Selkirk as well.

Again, not that Selkirk is a bad place, but from a demand standpoint, we need to understand what we are dealing with. Let's break down some vital statistics from the 2016 real estate year in Selkirk by looking at Figure 6.1 on the next page.

Figure 6.1: 2016 Final Real Estate Sales for the 12158 Zip Code of Selkirk, NY

Homes Listed	Homes Sold	% Sold	Avg Price	DOM
108	74	69%	$214,486	69

*Courtesy of the Eastern NY Regional Multiple Listing Service from 1/1/2016 to 12/31/2016

OK, wow. Selkirk (12158) is doing pretty well. But as we have learned in this book, there is more to this data than meets the eye. From these statistics only, we would figure that we have a 69% chance of a successful sale. That sale should also happen within 70 days, and average prices for this area are around $215,000.

108 homes listed for sale in the entire year is a considerably low-volume market. There isn't a lot of homes available to home buyers in Ravena, but you can at least expect a home with a decent sized lot. Regardless, the 74 home sales and 69% sale ratio is definitely encouraging, but of course, we must look further at the data and segment where needed.

SCHOOL DISTRICT

Once we have analyzed the zip codes real estate sales data, we need to learn more about how the school district performs. Overall we know that the Ravena-Coeymans school district is ranked 25th out of the 49 Capital Region School Districts I rank. Not bad.

Figure 6.2 on the following page shows us what the 2016 final real estate numbers looked like for all homes within the Ravena-Coeymans School District:

Figure 6.2: 2016 Final Real Estate Sales for the Ravena-Coeymans School District.

Homes Listed	Homes Sold	% Sold	Avg Price	DOM
242	148	61%	$170,943	81

Courtesy of the Eastern NY Regional Multiple Listing Service from 1/1/2016 to 12/31/2016

Immediately, we see that the Ravena-Coeymans School District covers more of a geographical area than just the 12158 Selkirk zip code does. The district ended 2016 with 242 homes available on the market, with 148 homes selling. That was a 61% success rate, with an average sale price of around $170,000, which took about 81 days to receive a contract.

The overall sale price is much lower in the district when compared to the Selkirk zip code. Homes were also taking longer to sell, and had a slightly smaller percentage of success at 61%.

But we must segment deeper now to understand how the market performs for homes in the Selkirk zip code of 12158, while combining with Ravena schools. Let's jump back to the zip code stats to see what is happening with the overall sales data.

Figure 6.3, on the next page, shows us the 2016 real estate sales data for the 12158 zip code, **when combined** with the Ravena-Coeymans school district.

Figure 6.3: 2016 Final Real Estate Sales for the 12158 Zip Code combined with Ravena-Coeymans School District.

Homes Listed	Homes Sold	% Sold	Avg. Price	DOM
86	59	69%	$201,500	75

Courtesy of the Eastern NY Regional Multiple Listing Service from 1/1/2016 to 12/31/2016

Now we are getting somewhere. We see that we are zeroed into the exact home we have to sell. 239 Beaver Dam Rd is in the 12158 zip code and pulls from Ravena-Coeymans schools. This is the data that we really need to look at first. If we didn't segment the data, we would be left with a skewed perspective that isn't accurate.

This is because the overall averages for 12158 also consisted of 15 home sales in 2016, which pulled from the Bethlehem School District, a Top 10 school district in our area according to my ranking system. You can see those numbers in Figure 6.4 below.

Figure 6.4: 2016 Final Real Estate Sales for the 12158 Zip Code combined with Bethlehem School District.

Homes Listed	Homes Sold	% Sold	Avg. Price	DOM
22	15	68%	$265,564	44

Courtesy of the Eastern NY Regional Multiple Listing Service from 1/1/2016 to 12/31/2016

Here we see 22 homes listed in 2016 which had a 12158 Selkirk address **and pulled** from Bethlehem schools. We see 15 of these 22 sellers sold their home in an average of just 44 days for an average price of $265,564. These are better numbers and final average sale prices when compared to the 12158 zip code alone, and better than the 12158 zip code when combined with the Ravena-Coeymans School District final sales data.

The Bethlehem School District owners in the 12158 zip code sold their homes faster and for more money based on the school district. If 239 Beaver Dam Road was located in Bethlehem Schools, we could have asked for more money in the sale.

Once we segment the data, we know what we are dealing with. We know that the Selkirk zip code is of low volume, but has decent demand. Average sale prices are at the region average of $200,000, and most sellers are getting it done within 90 days.

CONDITION

When it comes to condition on this particular home, it was a bit of a tougher process in that, the home is a Log style home, which are very rare in our area. So rare, in fact that in all of 2016, only 55 log homes were offered for sale on the market in the entire Capital Region. And by region, I mean the four main counties of Albany, Rensselaer, Saratoga, and Schenectady.

Luckily, the sales stats for Log homes were decent, but broad. What happens if we searched for all Log style home sales inside the 12158 zip code, with Ravena-Coeymans schools? The answer was zero. We would be the first. I like to bundle home style in with condition because it always starts with the home style, once we get location and school district out of the way.

The condition for 239 Beaver Dam Road was what I would consider good. As far as the structure goes, the home was on a cinderblock foundation. It had no issues with any shifting block or other common foundation issues that arise with cinderblock.

The basement was good for storage, but not a footprint that could be finished off. Plenty of room, but between the mechanical systems and other utilities, it would have been awkward to try and finish the basement.

The home itself was just 25 years old at the time. The roof had been replaced within the last 5 years, so that expense would be out of the buyers mind. The forced hot air furnace and central air condenser were each within 10 years old as well so, the buyer did not really have much to beat us up on apart from some maintenance issues. A radon gas test was performed, and passed.

Remember we were dealing with a Log style home as well. There comes a certain type of maintenance you have to keep up on when it comes to Log style homes. Carpenter bees love to drill holes in the outside boards and the sun likes to beat on those boards as well. Every handful of years, the owners would find themselves having the home stained, and/or replacing wood boards that were ruined by bees.

As with the exterior of the home, the interior walls were all wood. These required no upkeep, as they were stained and sealed upon construction and were not susceptible to the outside elements. The home did have some drywall in the kitchen and dining room, but for the most part, if you don't like Log homes and exposed wood galore, you're weren't going to like 239 Beaver Dam Road.

This was a big obstacle to overcome. Our buyer pool was very small. You have to love Log style homes in order to even schedule a showing on this property. Apart from the condition, the interior was a bit cluttered, and the owners were great to heed my advice and get a lot of things moved to storage. We needed to make the home seem bigger than it really was, which is always the goal in real estate. The floorplan of the home was split down the middle with a wall, so the 1,800+ square feet felt more like 1,500 square feet.

Nevertheless, we got the home looking more open, and shot some professional photos, as well as aerial drone shots of the property, and were able to present the home beautifully online. Remember, perception is reality when it comes to online marketing, and nice photos means it's a nice house in a home buyers mind. Since this home was already nice, the professional photos made it all the better.

TAXES

The overall taxes, without discounts included, was just south of $6,000. The new owner would expect to pay this much, and could pay less once discounts are applied. Overall, the tax amounts weren't terrible, but they weren't great either. Anytime you have a home that is not in a high demand location, having high taxes on top of it can make things even harder, and your overall sale price much lower.

Taxes are also important for folks who don't care about the school district. I know that schools are one of my Key Factors, however, a lot of folks never care what the school district is because they either have no kids, or their kids are grown and moved on. For our buyers, they planned on living the rest of their days in 239 Beaver Dam. It was their version of a retirement home, a Log style home with land, this was what they sought, thus, taxes became more important to them than the schools district itself.

TIMING

For us, timing was terrible, but as mentioned in this book, people move for different reasons. Health was the reason why my clients were selling a home they had raised their family in. The almost five acres was too much for them to keep up with, and they wanted to downsize, a common reason to sell and a pretty good one at that. But it was more than just downsizing. As noted, health was also a factor for my folks. They understood that November was not the best time to sell a home, but they needed to get out as soon as possible for their own health issues related to the upkeep, plus the health of their family members, who owned the home they planned on moving into next. Their family was on a time restraint, they had to move now. We needed to get the sale done at 239 Beaver Dam so the proceeds could go towards the next purchase before their family put that home on the market and sold it to whomever would bid.

With this being the case, and listing the home in November, I explained to these folks that price was everything. If you want to sell fast, heading into the holidays, we need to be aggressive on the price, but also realistic. This is all about coming to the best possible price for your home. They had the equity with 239 Beaver Dam, so how can we get the most out of it?

We quickly learned that we had a bit more time than we originally thought, their potential new home was safe from another home buyers grasp until after the holidays. We now knew we had at least 60 days, if not 90, to get it done. Without a choice, we hit the market just weeks before Thanksgiving.

THE SALE

We were live on November 6th, not the best time to be on the market in Selkirk. We knew where we stood with just 80+ homes listed per year when we combined school district with the zip code. I warned my clients early on that things would be slow at first, but we hoped for the best. The 5 Key Factors were weighed, and my suggested price was in and around $250,000. Of course, my sellers cringed a bit. With the acreage and uniqueness of the home, they wanted to push it closer to $270,000.

Something you should know about what it's like to work with me, I always deliver an in-depth and honest opinion about a home's value. I also tell my clients that, this (price) is what I believe to be the price based on the research of data, the time of year, and the other Key Factors in this book. Also, the seller's motive for selling and the time crunch we were feeling. Regardless, they are free to try their price, as long as we follow a strict schedule to decrease the price when things get quiet, and hopefully a schedule that coincides with a 90 day sale, tops.

Of course, this is not how you get a home sold quickly or for the most money, and I am not one for price deductions. But this is also a give-and-take industry. Who am I to not compromise with a home seller, even if I believe time will be wasted if a price is too high?

Knowing that we can at least see and adjust quickly usually helps folks feel better once the market speaks to us and our price, which is, in most cases, too high. So what did our price schedule look like? I'm not going to bore you with a complete story that involves every detail about the showings and the feedback. Let me instead use our pricing schedule to do a final analysis of this home sale. Take a look at our pricing schedule in Figure 6.5.

Figure 6.5: 239 Beaver Dam Rd. Home Sale Timeline

Date	Action	Price
11/06/2015	Listed for Sale	$268,000
2/9/2016	Price Drop	$258,000
3/13/2016	Offer accepted	$250,000
4/25/2016	Closed sale price	$250,000

The home was listed at $268,000 heading into the holidays and the wintertime. We were patient with price deductions for many reasons. Apart from the time of year, we knew from the statistics that Selkirk, and the Ravena-Coeymans markets were slow moving. Average days on market ranged from 70-90 days and about 100 homes sell every year, no matter how you slice the data.

We waited 90 days before we dropped the price. With a new asking price of $258,000, it took us just 30 more days for us to get an offer. We settled on a $250,000 sale price from buyers that were "watching the home online for a while". By April 2016, we saw a closing table. It took 127 days to get a contract, but considering the time of year and the lower demand area, this wasn't too bad.

So what do you think? Could more money had been made if starting at $250,000? The List Price to Sale Price ratio statistic, discussed in the Introduction of this book, tells us that on average, we can expect anywhere from 95% to 100% of our asking price, depending on the area of the region. For us, we landed just about 97% of our asking price of $258,000 and 93% of our original asking price of $268,000, in 120+ days. It's probably accurate to say that we could have gotten the same amount for the home at any time of the year, if we started at $250,000. Sure some folks could has always offered less than $250,000 if we actually started there, but most likely, we would have received full price of $250,000 if we listed the home in the Spring.

All in all our price points were accurate. My $250,000 suggested starting point was based on the 5 Key Factors described in this book. It was also determined by more in-depth research of the local market, and the motivation of the home seller. Once they had realized they had some more time than they thought, we raised our expectations and tried to get more money with a starting price of $268,000. With only having to drop the price once to get an offer, I would say we did good.

I hope all my sellers get above and beyond the price they expect for their home, but that is usually not the case. Sure, we ended up selling where I suggested, but we lost three months of time trying for a higher price. Of course, based on the data analysis, 239 Beaver Dam was a home located in an area of lower demand, a unique home style, and topped it off with some tough timing. But in the end, we got it sold, which is the obvious goal.

You may think this Case Study is a bit contradictory to some of my theories and beliefs laid out in this book so far, and I won't disagree with you. I mean, didn't I say all homes should sell in 90 days, and overpricing the home, plus listing it in the Winter means losing time and money? Yes, and I stand by that.

But again, the reason is simple. I am just an advisor in the sale of your home. Even though my sellers here at 239 Beaver Dam Road wanted and needed to sell quickly, they still couldn't bring themselves to budge off their higher asking price. Many sellers get stuck believing that their home is worth more than it is. While I can only present the facts and data on the market, I still need my clients to consider taking my guidance.

Obviously, I cannot twist a sellers arm and force them to price their home where I suggest. Sometimes a home seller takes the long way to the sale, instead of the four-lane highway with no traffic. Even when sellers have to sell their home by tomorrow, they still get caught up on trying for a price that is usually unlikely. I can only open the doors, the home sellers have to walk through them.

CASE STUDY #2

By Ryan Hoffman

Address: 53 Rooney Ave. Albany, NY

Zip Code: 12205

Zip Code Rank: 5th out of 70

School District: South Colonie

School District Rank: 3rd out of 49

THE DETAILS

53 Rooney Ave is a 3 bedroom, 1 bathroom, Ranch style home. It had around 1,000 square feet of living space and it has just a crawl space for the foundation as opposed to a full basement. The home was located on a flat, square lot. While it did have a fenced in yard, the lot was small and was located on a street with other homes that had similar sized yards. Features worth mentioning were some upgrades to the kitchen, laminate flooring, and some new hardwood in the living room. The furnace and all the windows were also improved.

Let's breakdown the story of how this home lined up with the 5 Key Factors and ultimately, how we got this home sold.

LOCATION

53 Rooney is located is the highly popular, and very busy, 12205 zip code known as Colonie (Albany). The 12205 zip code currently ranks 5th overall out of the 70 zip codes I cover. The popularity of this zip code is obvious when you begin to break down some of its features.

The 12205 zip code stretches from around Exit 5 off of Interstate 90, down Central Ave towards Schenectady and also includes neighborhoods in and around Wolf Rd. People can take advantage of an easy commute, and an amenity filled lifestyle when living in Colonie. With the Northway, or Interstate 90, you can commute to many places within minutes of the 12205 zip code. And of course with Colonie Center and Wolf Rd, there is no shortage of things to do, places to eat, and stores to spend your money in. Of course with views of the Albany skyline on Central Ave, commuters love this close proximity to the state capital buildings as well.

It's no surprise why the 12205 zip code is popular. But what about the real estate stats in this market? Here is where demand really shines through. Figure 7.1 shows us the 2016 final housing market stats for the 12205 zip code.

Figure 7.1: 2016 Final Real Estate Sales for the 12205 Zip Code of Colonie, NY

Homes Listed	Homes Sold	% Sold	Avg Price	DOM
361	291	80%	$182,357	51

*Courtesy of the Eastern NY Regional Multiple Listing Service from 1/1/2016 to 12/31/2016

Colonie is no stranger to popularity, and the real estate stats prove this. 291 homes sold in 2016, compared to the 361 home listed for sale. With an 80% success rate, buyers would have needed to act quickly, especially with an average days on market of just 51 days.

The average sale price in Colonie is also the most affordable when talking about the Top 10 real estate markets in our area. It is a great place for a starter home, or to downsize. With Ranch style homes dominating this landscape, we learn why the average sale price is under $200,000. But we will get to that later.

361 homes listed in one year is not a slow market. While it cannot top the 700+ homes we see listed in Clifton Park and Saratoga Springs, Colonie is still able to rank as a Top 5 market when listing nearly half the homes as the #1 and #2 ranked markets do.

There is a pretty good success rate of selling when you're looking at 80% averages. And it's worth mentioning that in 2016, sellers also averaged 97.66% of their asking price in Colonie.

Colonie has a great geographic location, at an affordable price, but the area has even more going for it than this. They back up the great location, by pulling from a top ranked school district, the South Colonie Central School District.

SCHOOL DISTRICT

The South Colonie School District ranks 3rd overall among the 49 school districts I cover. This is a big deal. Remember, I rank school districts in order of leverage, or demand, based on the real estate statistics talked about in this book. We will see in Figure 7.2 why the South Colonie School District is ranked so high when looking at their 2016 final numbers.

Figure 7.2: 2016 Final Real Estate Sales for the South Colonie School District.

Homes Listed	Homes Sold	% Sold	Avg Price	DOM
538	434	81%	$197,694	48

Courtesy of the Eastern NY Regional Multiple Listing Service from 1/1/2016 to 12/31/2016

In an average of just 48 days, 434 homes sold for an average sale price of $197,694. With an 81% sale ratio on homes listed vs. sold, this clearly indicates high demand.

As always, we combine the school district sales, with the zip code sales, as a way to get the final statistical picture that relates best for 53 Rooney Ave. For your reference, Figure 7.3 shows the 2016 real estate sales data for the 12205 zip code, when combined with the South Colonie school district. See Figure 7.3 on the next page.

Figure 7.3: 2016 Final Real Estate Sales for the 12205 Zip Code combined with the South Colonie School District.

Homes Listed	Homes Sold	% Sold	Avg. Price	DOM
346	275	80%	$187,224	45

Courtesy of the Eastern NY Regional Multiple Listing Service from 1/1/2016 to 12/31/2016

Notice how the school district alone is listing more homes overall than the zip code itself of 12205. This is because school districts encompass many different zip codes. As I mentioned before in this book, it's crucial to see these numbers in an effort to drill down and see what is causing the success, and demand, inside the market.

We are seeing that not many homes dropped off when compared to our first look at the school district overall. This is because the majority of 12205 home owners pull from South Colonie schools, while just a handful of other 12205 owners pull from Albany and North Colonie schools. We do see a quicker sale by 5 days, and even an extra $5,000 in the sale price when comparing the South Colonie School Distrct data to the zip code data of 12205. Again, it is so crucial to segment down and look at the data as it pertains to the homes zip code and school district combined.

When it comes to Location and School District, 53 Rooney Ave looked like a solid opportunity for the home owner to squeeze every penny out of the sale. We have high demand from the onset, so let's see what else this home had going for it.

CONDITION

As mentioned, the Colonie area in general consists mostly of Ranch style homes. Built in the 1950's, post WWII era, a time when housing was in high demand for the baby boomers, which were starting to rise in population and would continue to do so into the 1960's.

In all honesty, the condition was a bit sub-par. The best features of the home consisted of the new hardwoods in the living room, but the rest of the home flooring was finished with a miss-matched laminate flooring and other drawbacks.

The kitchen was small, but was upgraded with stock cabinetry and laminate counter tops. There was a dining table, but trying to seat more than two people was a stretch. With no dining room at all, that always creates a drawback in the mind of home buyers. Where could they entertain guests?

With just under 1,000 square feet, and small bedrooms, the home was somewhat of a tough sell even though there is such high demand in the South Colonie School District.

Some of the detail work throughout the home was lacking as well. Closet doors were missing, some outlets were loose and the outlet covers were hanging off. This may not seem like a big deal, but a simple fix left neglected, gives potential home buyers the idea that the rest of the home needs work. The attic space was good for storage, but nothing else, and the crawl space in the basement was only accessible through an oversized window on the outside of the foundation wall. Other perks included a roof that still had life in it, and newer windows throughout.

One other major drawback was the recalled electrical panel. It was a model that was old and prone to being a fire hazard. This was disclosed and a concern for would be home buyers. Not only was it a hazard, but some insurance companies won't issue a policy on a home with an electrical panel of this kind.

53 Rooney Ave definitely had some challenges, and the market would prove to speak at us about these issues in regards to condition.

TAXES

The taxes on 53 Rooney Ave were very affordable. I let my seller know that this is important to factor since a home buyers payment will also become more affordable.

The overall taxes, without discounts included, was just $3,100 per year. This is one of the main reasons why the Colonie area performs so well. They boast some of the lowest taxes for property owners within the four main counties. This allows home owners to ask more money for their homes than what a similar size home would fetch in an area with say, double the taxes. With just $3,100 to worry about per year in taxes and average sale prices under $200,000, Colonie and the South Colonie School District will continue to see high demand and good sales as long as the lower taxes last.

TIMING

In this case, timing was great for 53 Rooney. We listed the home almost on the best day we possible could; April 30th. With May being the peak listing season (June is strong too), we were really lining up the 5 Key Factors in textbook fashion.

You cannot ask for better timing to list a home for sale, especially in a Top 5 market. But the homes condition would come back to bite us in the end. Let's take a look at how the overall sale shook out.

THE SALE

For my seller, timeframe wasn't all that important. The home was technically vacant, and thus easy to show to other agents and home buyers. The seller and her husband had already purchased another home in Niskayuna, so while they still had to pay the mortgage and utilities, it wasn't so urgent where we needed a sale within the week.

Of course all home sellers want to sell their home for the most money, in the least amount of time on the market, which is possible, but only when the starting price is correct.

In our case, I explained what type of demand the Colonie and South Colonie markets had. I also segmented the sales data down to Ranch style homes, and found that average sale prices for a Ranch home in 12205 combined with South Colonie schools, was around $160,000 at the time.

Turns out that the average sale prices in Colonie for Ranch homes that had a full basement, compared to Ranch homes that did not have a full basement, showed a difference of about $35,000. Have a look for yourself in Figure 7.4.

Figure 7.4: 2015 Ranch Sales in 12205 + South Colonie Schools. Slab vs Full Basement

Slab/Crawl Space	$137,697
Full Basement	$173,080

Courtesy of the Eastern NY Regional Multiple Listing Service from 1/1/2015 to 12/31/2015

It would take another 100+ pages to explain all the angles I take when pricing a home. Not only is it a combination of these 5 Key Factors, it also consists of a 21 point checklist of attributes inside the home that need to be considered. In the case of 53 Rooney Ave, the lack of basement and the condition of the home overall, ended up hurting us in the end.

My seller was pretty confident about the sale. Unfortunately, she was too confident. In this case, and often in other situations I am in, sellers often quote a recent home sale in their neighborhood that they deem as an accurate comparison to their home. But it comes down to so many different features and benefits inside a home, that one single sale cannot be used to determine your price. Figure 7.5 shows our price schedule for 53 Rooney Ave.

The timeline is not what you would expect for a home located in a top market, especially since we received over 70 showings from agents before we got an offer. Let's see where we went wrong, and how we finally closed the deal.

Figure 7.5: 53 Rooney Ave. Home Sale Timeline

Date	Action	Price
04/30/2016	Listed for sale	$168,000
6/10/2016	Price Drop	$158,000
7/14/2016	Price Drop	$148,000
8/29/2016	Offer accepted	$128,960
11/07/2016	Closed sale price	$128,960

So where did we go wrong? Personally, I thought an asking price of $150,000 was a good starting point. But again, based on home owners wishes, and being seduced a bit by the high demand market, we decided to go for the absolute top price point of $168,000.

We quickly learned that the market was in as much high demand as the statistics indicate. We had over 70 showings on this home in 90 days.

We literally almost averaged one new showing per day for three months. But the majority of the feedback was that the home was overpriced with too much work needed. Home buyers, and their agents, commented about the interior detail work that needed to be fixed, and also, the lack of a formal dining room and lack of a full basement.

The house was small, as were the bedrooms, but with great professional photos, and a great high demand market, the showings never really stopped. With this being the case, my seller was willing to be patient since activity was so high. Even with some bad feedback, the seller was also willing to wait as long as possible before dropping the price.

We waited just over one month before coming down $10,000 on our price to $158,000. After the same negative feedback kept coming in while still having a high amount of showings, we dropped the price again to $148,000, and this was good enough to get us an offer.

We spent 116 days on the market before receiving an offer. However, that offer came 45 days after the price drop to $148,000, which is where we could have started three months prior. It is worth mentioning that we did have an offer in the $150,000's at one point but both sides couldn't come to terms on a deal. In hindsight, my seller should have accepted this offer, but of course, you never know if that deal would have made it all the way to the closing table. Nevertheless, we finally got the home sold for just about $129,000.

The seller sold for under 90% list price vs. sale price ratio. Something that only happens when the price is too high. Even at $148,000, we still needed 45 days before we received an offer. And at a $129,000 sale price, we should have been listed for say $135,000 to begin with.

Which reminds me of the statistics on page 120 where Figure 7.4 showed the different sale prices between Ranch homes with and without full basements. The $137,000+ average sale price of Ranch homes without full basements proved to be the reality based on our overall final sale price.

High demand and a ton of action, plus a missed offer, may have skewed our mindset a bit here. Again, I am always trying to give my honest opinion on price, more-so based on data than opinion. Some sellers are adamant about what they want to try and get for their home and have a hard time trusting real estate agents, for good reasons.

This is why sales data can tell us the true story of how we can sell a home, rather than relying on opinions, or shallow research that uses just a few comps.

We sold 53 Rooney for 96% of $135,000. Constant feedback and endless showings also told us a tale of being priced to high. In the end though, the home seller is in control. If advice is taken with more confidence, the timeline for a sale can be moved up without jeopardizing the bottom line. What we learned with 53 Rooney is that, we can have a home located in a top demand area, with a top school district, and still not sell it in the timeframe we expect. You have to weigh the condition of the home more heavily, as well as listen to the story the market tells us. With so many Ranch sales in Colonie, we had a lot of other similar sales that can be used for comparison, but we must analyze closely. The numbers don't lie.

DEFEND YOUR EQUITY

CASE STUDY #3

By Ryan Hoffman

Address: 16 Drummer Dr. Mechanicville, NY

Zip Code: 12118

Zip Code Rank: 18th out of 70

School District: Mechanicville

School District Rank: 27th out of 49

THE DETAILS

16 Drummer Drive is what I considered to be a Colonial style home. It was only seven years old, built new by my clients in 2010. Considering its modern design, it was more of a Colonial style home combined with a Contemporary style home. Determining the category of a home style is important for dissecting the market statistics more accurately and this modern home was sort of a hybrid that did not fit into a category of home styles I was used to. More on why this became important in a bit.

The home featured 4 bedrooms and 2.5 bathrooms. It was advertised as 2,050 square feet and also had a two car garage. As noted, it was a young home, so as you can imagine, it featured a lot of modern touches. Hardwood flooring on the first floor, and carpeting on the 2nd floor. It also had carpeting in a finished basement area. Although I was surprised with the laminate counter tops the builder put in, overall, the next home buyer had little to do but move into this one.

Let's breakdown the story of how this home lined up with the 5 Key Factors, and ultimately, how we got this home sold.

LOCATION

The 12118 zip code is a combination of the 100+ year old City of Mechanicville, and newer construction developments as you head north up the hill towards Stillwater. It is also a zip code that is known for having some home sales that pull from the Shenendehowa School District, my #1 ranked School District out of the 49 school districts in my rankings. With close proximity to Clifton Park and other Saratoga County locations, Mechanicville has been favorable to home sellers in recent years.

At the time of our listing endeavor, both the 12118 zip code and Mechanical School District markets were considered seller markets with absorption rates above the 20% mark needed to be deemed as such. Let's look at Figure 8.1 for the 2016 statistics in the 12118 zip code and see how the market had performed.

Figure 8.1: 2016 Final Real Estate Sales for the 12118 Zip Code of Mechanicville, NY

Homes Listed	Homes Sold	% Sold	Avg Price	DOM
215	124	58%	$282,892	67

Courtesy of the Eastern NY Regional Multiple Listing Service from 1/1/2016 to 12/31/2016

Not bad numbers by any means. A 200+ homes listed campaign in 2016, but with just 58% of those homes selling? What made me scratch my head even more was, the average sale price pushing $300,000? How could it be so high with homes selling at under a 60% rate? Could it be the majority of homes are overpriced in this zip code? That's likely. Or could it be that more expensive homes just take longer to sell sometimes, especially when the school district isn't a Top 5 or a Top 10 district. The fact that we are asking these questions at all is a positive step in the right direction.

This is why when I am looking at zip code stats, I always pull the school districts that are within these zip codes. Figure 8.2 shows us what the 12118 zip code housing stats looked like at the end of 2016, but segmented by school districts. See Figure 8.2 on the next page.

Figure 8.2: 2016 Final Real Estate Sales for the 12118 Zip Code, Segmented by School District

School	Homes Listed	Homes Sold	% Sold	Avg Price	DOM
Mechanicville	128	65	51%	$211,992	49
Shenendehowa	68	47	69%	$382,554	94
Stillwater	18	11	61%	$274,500	65

We see right away why the 12118 zip code numbers looked a bit askew. The 47 homes that sold, in which the sellers pulled from the Shenendehowa School District, had inflated the overall averages inside the 12118 zip code drastically. Average sale prices for Shenendehowa sellers inside 12118 were closer to $400,000 while Mechanicville School District sellers were closer to the $200,000 price range, in the same zip code.

Geographically, I can see why the 12118 area can be somewhat desirable. Obviously it's close enough to Clifton Park where a chunk of home owners actually send their kids to Shenendehowa, but you also have close proximity to all things Saratoga County. Commuting for a day at the race track, or SPAC, isn't terrible, whether it be by way of Route 9 or the Northway and Round Lake and Malta are also very close.

You can also get down to Rensselaer County via Route 4/Hudson River Road, which can get you into Waterford and closer to 787 in about 15-20 minutes. Of course you can cross the river, in just seconds, to other parts of Rensselaer County, but nothing to notable there besides

Schaghticoke and routes to Vermont. It borders up to the Hudson River, and its location, while isn't the most convenient, does have its perks.

Overall we see that just looking at the averages for the zip code only, would have given us an unrealistic picture of what we were working with. And we also had to depend on the homes overall age, to get us a better idea of what price a seven year old could fetch in growing market that still had 100+ year old homes selling in it.

SCHOOL DISTRICT

Before we get to the details, let's take a look at the Mechanicville School District housing market statistics for 2016. I already sort of spoiled you with some school district statistics inside the 12118 zip code, and we know where we stand. But let's see what the overall demand is for what I deem only the 27th best school district in our area. Figure 8.3 depicts the sales information for all of 2016 inside Mechanicville schools.

Figure 8.3: 2016 Final Real Estate Sales for the Mechanicville School District.

Homes Listed	Homes Sold	% Sold	Avg. Price	DOM
139	77	55%	$216,271	53

Courtesy of the Eastern NY Regional Multiple Listing Service from 1/1/2016 to 12/31/2016

The majority of the 12118 zip code consists of Mechanicville Schools, apart from a dozen or so that pull from Stillwater, and Shenendehowa schools, we can see these numbers are pretty similar to the zip codes stats themselves.

It's still just over a 50-50 shot of selling a home in the Mechanicville School District. And a slightly above-average sale price of $216,271 is a bit dismal especially when considering we are dealing with a home that's not even seven years old yet.

This information can only take us so far. Once we get into condition, we start to segment by home style and age of home. Mechanicville Schools and its zip code are not the greatest, nor are they the worst when it comes to demand, it's more of an even playing field. We must understand our state within the market before we go out there asking for a Shenendehowa School price and not a Mechanicville School price for the home. We see a difference of almost $200,000 in average sale prices when it comes to Shenendehowa sales vs. Mechanicville sales, so this particular home was quite a challenge for the market since younger homes can often be overpriced.

CONDITION

Of course, looking at homes still being built brand new was a reference point for us in this one. There were literally four or five new homes sites being built in this same development when we listed 16 Drummer Drive. This is crucial when you're in this situation because if buyers see us asking the same price, or more, for a seven year old home compared to a home they could buy brand new, we know we cannot expect much action.

But when it came to condition, what more could you ask for in a seven year old home? I mean the roof, the furnace, everything, is just seven years old. It's more or less, maintenance free for the first 10 years a new buyer moves in. I know, barring something major that goes wrong, and things often go wrong inside a home, but in all honesty, you have to feel better about the sale with such a young home. I mean, it's hardly even been lived in.

The only thing that was stopping us from selling was being overpriced, and we know how common that is. I had to look inside the 124 home sales in the 12118 zip code to see what the difference was between the older home sales and the new home sales. And I found some good news.

I searched for all sales in 2016 that consisted of homes with ages under ten years old. What I saw was 45 home sales inside 12118 had been homes that fit this criteria. That was almost 40% of the market share! The average sale price for these 45 sales came in at $370,000. That was also great news for us.

But I took it one step further. I segmented down to just Colonial home style sales only, and the results, of course, differed again. In fact, no matter how many times and ways you segment, the average sale prices differed. The good news was, we were in the $300,000 range regardless.

16 Drummer Drive really only had two drawbacks. Again, this Colonial hybrid style home was laid out differently than a typical Colonial home you may be thinking of. With a standard Colonial (or center hall Colonial), you enter the front door and can usually go right, or left to enter different rooms of the home. Usually there may be a den to your right, then a hallway with a half bath down the middle. The half bath is usually under the stairs, and then the hall continues into the kitchen. To the left of the stairs, in most cases, you can enter a dining room or living room. But that was not the case with us. Obviously, builders are getting more creative, trying to design some hybrid type floor plans.

See Figure 8.4 on the next page for a view of a typical Colonial floorplan that I am referring to, and we can see the difference between this classic style and the floor plan we were dealing with at 16 Drummer Drive.

Figure 8.4: Classic Colonial floorplan

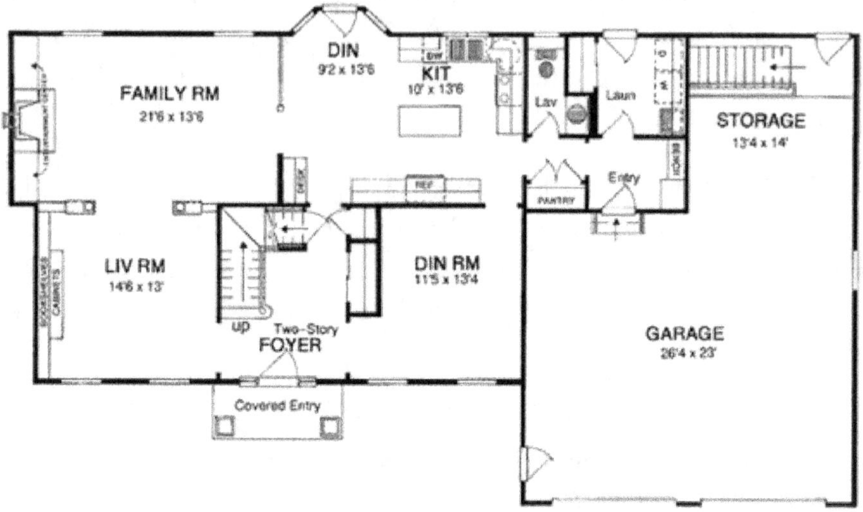

16 Drummer Drive had a different type of floorplan than that of the classic Colonial style we see in Figure 8.4. The stairs were butted up to the right, and you could only enter straight into the kitchen. The 1st floor consisted of a Kitchen, Dining Room and a Living Room, with a half bath and access to the garage. The 2nd floor consisted of all 4 bedrooms and 2 full bathrooms.

On the next page, Figure 8.5 shows us the floorplan for 16 Drummer Drive and the obvious differences when compared to a classic Colonial style home.

Figure 8.5: 16 Drummer Drive floorplan

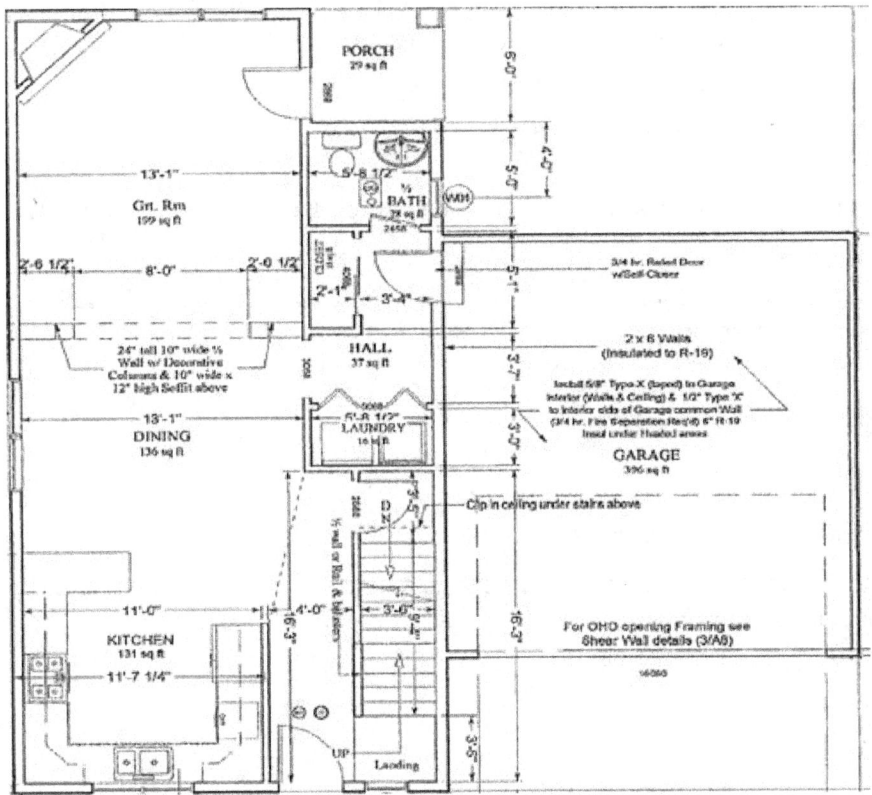

This had definitely deterred some buyers. The home is laid out in a rectangle shape, as compared to the square shape of a standard Colonial. This lack of flow was one negative aspect that would hurt our sale.

The other issue was the yard. There was a steep drop off behind the home, which fell into a natural creek. The rest of the yard spread out to the side of the home, and folks don't really want to hang out in the side yard. With just a small section of yard available behind the home for use, this turned off interested home buyers with children and pets. There wasn't any real room to run around with the family.

The yard, and the layout of the home are always included features when I talk about condition. These features make a big difference in the sale and how much you can get for your home. As you will see in Figure 8.6, it surely hurt us a bit. See some of the feedback we received that shows how the yard became the main issue for potential home buyers. Please excuse the clarity of these images as they are not official pictures and had to be copied off of a web page.

Figure 8.6: Screenshots of agent feedback from 16 Drummer Drive showings.

Is your client interested in this listing?	Not interested
Please rate your overall experience at this showing.	Excellent
Your (and your client's) opinion of the price:	Too high
Please rate this listing (5=Best; 1=Worst):	4
COMMENTS/RECOMMENDATIONS:	This is a beautiful, well maintained home. Unfortunately the yard size is a deal breaker for them.

Is your client interested in this listing?	Maybe
Please rate your overall experience at this showing.	Good
Your (and your client's) opinion of the price:	
Please rate this listing (5=Best; 1=Worst):	4
COMMENTS/RECOMMENDATIONS:	back yard little small

Is your client interested in this listing?	Somewhat
Please rate your overall experience at this showing.	Excellent
Your (and your client's) opinion of the price:	Too high
Please rate this listing (5=Best; 1=Worst):	4
COMMENTS/RECOMMENDATIONS:	They like the floor plan very much. Yard is a little small. They are discussing

Apart from the yard, the interior of the home was immaculate. With the home being just seven years old, the interior features were practically brand new. There literally were no issues a home buyer had to worry about with this home. It really just came down to pricing the home at a point that reflected the drawbacks of the lot. Before we get to the details of the sale, let's talk about the taxes.

TAXES

The overall taxes, without discounts included, were around $6,700 per year. Of course, this wasn't great news. I mean, having a seven year old home seems like an easy sale, but the higher your taxes are, the lower your sale price gets. Not to mention, the $300,000 price point begins to shrink your qualified buyer pool as well.

For Drummer Drive, the stage was set. Marketing the home with taxes that are pushing $7,000 isn't fun and the fact is, the asking price must be adjusted accordingly. In this case, my final opinion on price wasn't going to be a fun conversation to have with my home selling clients. Especially because they had already been on the market for sale with another agent prior to me picking up the listing.

TIMING

We had some good timing on our side as we were set to list the home in March, this of course was after the home already failed to sell a few months prior with another agent, and this information came with some additional strings attached.

My new clients at 16 Drummer Drive had already spent 120 days on the market with another agent. Granted, they listed in November of 2016 with that agent, a terrible month to list your home for sale as we know. What made things worse was the fact that the agent overpriced the home with a $334,000 initial asking price. They only dropped the price once, to $324,000, before pulling the home from the market in February 2017. But the stress didn't stop there.

The owners of 16 Drummer Drive had trusted their former agent to sell their home and have him represent them on a new home purchase as well. They were under contract to buy a new home in Clifton Park with this agent, which was now theirs to lose since 16 Drummer Drive failed to sell the first time on the market. This is what is known as a 48 hour contingency. If you have ever wondered how buying a new home, and selling your current home can be accomplished simultaneously, this is how it works. Even though the owners of 16 Drummer Drive were able to get an offer accepted on a new home purchase, it was contingent upon 16 Drummer Drive getting a contract of their own.

Without a buyer at 16 Drummer Drive, these nice folks would lose their dream home purchase due to being overpriced and failing to sell. As noted, the $324,000 asking price wasn't getting it done at 16 Drummer Drive.

These folks decided to cut ties with their listing agent, even though this agent was still representing them as a buyers agent on the 48 hour contingent contract for their dream home in Clifton Park. Now, it was on me, as the new listing agent, to get 16 Drummer Drive sold, so they could solidify the deal for the Clifton Park home.

Upon my first meeting with these folks, and the fact that they could still try and salvage the new purchase in Clifton Park, I recommended listing the home at $299,000. A $25,000 deduction, with me as the new listing agent, wasn't really getting them excited. So, we settled on a new asking price of $318,500, even though I vocalized the fact that this was not good enough to get an offer.

THE SALE

We went live on March 18th, 2017 with a list price of $318,500. Snow still covered the ground, and the buying public had already seen this home on the market in prior months, so we had to be aware that this could be a potential drawback. I had stated that coming down just $5,500 on the asking price from the prior asking price of $324,000 wasn't enough to entice an offer. But since they still had a chance to satisfy the 48 hour contingency for the new home purchase, and needed all the money they could get, and they held out hope that an offer for over $300,000 was possible.

While we did have a few showing right away, for the most part, it was quiet. This is where studying the market is so crucial towards putting home seller stress at ease. We have a Mechanicville School District and overall area, that is favorable to home sellers at the time, but, is still low volume and somewhat of a slower market. Plus, there were competing homes for sale in this same housing development, thus, having an inflated price ended up hurting the sellers goals to satisfy the new purchase contract on their dream home in Clifton Park.

As you may have assumed by now, they lost out on their dream home which was still under contract with their former listing agent, and lucky for them, they lost that agent all together. With a 48 hour contingency, the sellers of that home in Clifton Park were able to field other offers from home buyers that did not have a home to sell. It was now back to square one for my clients at Drummer Drive to find their next dream home to purchase, which would still be contingent upon us selling.

Since they now had to start over and find another home, it altered our timeframe. We were no longer concerned with being overpriced, or in a hurry to drop the price, due to the fact that we had to get out into the Clifton Park market, schedule showings as home buyers, and find them a home they wanted to move to. Once they did, we would get aggressive with our asking price and drop the price on 16 Drummer Drive accordingly so we could get an offer and avoid the heartbreak they felt from the prior deal they lost.

If you have ever had to sell your home and buy a new one simultaneously, you know what a juggling act it can be. With one sale contingent upon the other, there are so many moving parts and the worry of it all falling though, it's enough to drive anyone crazy. And this was the situation we were in. Although not new to me at all, this was brand new to my folks. Considering they were already misled by their last agent, and missed out on a home they fell in love with, things were beginning to get a bit stressful. But in the end we got it done. Let's take a look at our pricing schedule and see how we did overall in the sale. Figure 8.7 lays out our timeline for the sale of 16 Drummer Drive.

Figure 8.7: 16 Drummer Dr. Home Sale Timeline

Date	Action	Price
3/18/2017	Listed for sale	$318,500
4/6/2017	Price Drop	$313,500
6/24/2017	Offer accepted	$290,000
8/5/2017	Closed sale price	$290,000

We ending up selling the home for around 92% of our asking price. This is indicative of selling a home that is overpriced. With the regions average around 97%, taking five points less when it came to list price versus sale price ratio, the market proved to see our inflated price, but were lucky enough to get an offer anyway. The home went under contract 88 days from the time we listed it. It's important to realize that seeing a 92% sale price versus list price ratio does not mean we had lost money, but simply that we were overpriced. The regions average of 97% just tells us that when a home is priced <u>correctly</u> it receives close to asking price. And when a home is overpriced, it receives less than the 97% average, which in this case, was 92%. All this means in the end is that our asking price should have been $299,000, seeing how 97% of $299,000 comes out to be $290,030, and that was just $30 off of the offer we accepted in the end.

Good communication with the buyer's agent in this case also helped our situation. Since most of the buying public saw us as an overpriced listing, I had to explain to the buyer's agent, that the sellers at 16 Drummer Drive were in the midst of buying a new home and that is why we hadn't dropped the price. I told the buyer's agent that we were aware that our price of $313,500 was too high and we planned to drop it anyway, and this communication made it possible for the reluctant home buyers to make an offer.

In real estate, you'd be surprised how hesitant home buyers and agents are when it comes to making an offer on a home that is overpriced. Without communicating openly about our awareness that we were in fact, overpriced, we may not have received an offer unless we officially dropped it to $299,000.

Looking back I think that all things happen for a reason. The new home my clients ended up buying was a bigger home, for less money, compared to the first home they lost out on.

In the case of 16 Drummer Drive, my clients were misled by an unqualified agent who had no price strategy and led them aimlessly through the market for 120 days. Selling a home always comes down to price, and usually it's much lower than home sellers expect. This is why market data and statistics are crucial to achieving your goals.

DEFEND YOUR EQUITY

CASE STUDY #4

By Ryan Hoffman

Address: 9 Mason St. Troy, NY

Zip Code: 12180

Zip Code Rank: 20th out of 70

School District: Troy

School District Rank: 22nd out of 49

THE DETAILS

9 Mason Street is a 4 bedroom, 1.5 bathroom Raised Ranch home located in Troy. It had 1,486 square feet of living space and featured a 1-car garage. This home was set up on a cul-de-sac and featured one of the bigger lots in the neighborhood.

If you're not familiar with a Raised Ranch style home, it typically features a split floor plan in which the "basement" is actual living space. This allows the square footage on the ground level to be counted in the floorplan when pertaining to a bank appraisal.

At 50 years old, this was no modern home. The owner had raised her family there and lived in the home for 35+ years. Now alone, the owner needed to sell the family property and was going to downsize to a condominium.

What is great about this case study is the fact that this home displays a perfect example of a clean and neat home, which has not been upgraded in many years. As I spoke about in the chapter regarding condition, to sell your home for the most money, quickly, all without having to do any major upgrades or repairs, is possible.

In the case of 9 Mason Street, the home was clean and well kept, but showed outdated features. The lower level carpeting and fixtures, including half bath, were dated back to the 1990's. The furnace and water heater had been upgraded at some point in the last 20 years, but it wasn't anything that was recent. The electrical panel, while an older model, was still up to code and modern building standards.

The kitchen was expanded during a construction project back in the 1980's, so it did have enough room to accommodate a 6-person dining table easily. The counter tops and cabinets were dated from the 1990's but overall the home was well kept, clutter free and clean. This is important.

Let's breakdown the story of how this home lined up with the 5 Key

Factors, and ultimately, how we got this home sold.

LOCATION

9 Mason Street was located in the high volume, Troy zip code of 12180. The Troy real estate market, and the 12180 zip code is actually a large geographic area. It encompasses the entire City of Troy, including parts southeast into Wynantskill and North Greenbush, and also pushes northeast as far as Pittstown.

With this being the reality, we often see the 12180 zip code putting up a lot of home sales every year. Let's take a look at Figure 9.1 to see how the 12180 Troy zip code scored after the 2016 year was complete.

Figure 9.1: 2016 Final Real Estate Sales for the 12180 Zip Code of Troy, NY

Homes Listed	Homes Sold	% Sold	Avg Price	DOM
491	363	74%	$167,302	79

*Courtesy of the Eastern NY Regional Multiple Listing Service from 1/1/2016 to 12/31/2016

We see that almost 500 homes hit the market in the 12180 zip code for the entire year of 2016. With 363 homes selling in comparison, the Troy zip code fared well for itself in what is typically an even market, favoring neither buyers nor sellers.

We see an average sale price that is below the Capital Region average of $200,000. This helps drive sales, of course, due to affordability, but the 79 days on market average is a bit surprising given the 74% success rate sellers were having.

There is no parity in the Troy zip code. Due to its geographic vastness, these 363 sales consist of everything from 100+ year old single family buildings in the city, to 50 year old country homes in Brunswick. This is why segmenting down to home style and age, is so important.

Apart from the statistical proof on how the zip code, as a whole is performing, the City of Troy and the 12180 zip code is one of the oldest areas in our region, yet still somewhat popular. Of course, with close access to 787, in some parts, it really isn't a bad commuter location. You can still get to many areas of our region in under 30 minutes from Troy. The one thing Rensselaer County lacks, overall, is a wide array of shopping and other amenities that seem to be readily available in areas like Latham, Clifton Park and even Albany.

Like all places, many folks with a history of family in Troy, usually stay in the area, or at least in Rensselaer County. While it is a more affordable market, recent tax hikes have dipped sale prices and turned off home buyers.

Adding to this discussion on 9 Mason Streets location, it was located in a planned urban development (neighborhood) that saw new construction from the 1960's through the 1990's. Point being, it was one of the more well-known and popular neighborhoods in the Troy area, and very familiar to the folks with a long history in Troy.

This allowed us to have immediate comparable sales within the neighborhood itself. Without needing to search the entire zip code for sales, it gave us a more detailed approach, and allowed us to price the home in a way that a bank appraiser would use to approve a mortgage on the property.

Overall, it was good enough to rank 20th overall in my zip code rankings, so let's see how the Troy School District fared in relation to the Troy zip code numbers.

SCHOOL DISTRICT

The Troy School District was also good enough to get a decent ranking with the list of 49 school districts I rank. At 22nd overall, the 12180 zip code, being as big as it is, finds some home owners being located in a few other school districts around Rennselaer County.

Let's see how the numbers looked after the 2016 campaign for all home sellers that sold within the Troy School District. See Figure 9.2.

Figure 9.2: 2016 Final Real Estate Sales for the Troy School District.

Homes Listed	Homes Sold	% Sold	Avg Price	DOM
299	223	75%	$142,763	81

*Courtesy of the Eastern NY Regional Multiple Listing Service from 1/1/2016 to 12/31/2016

Notice how the homes listed, and sold, within the Troy School District dropped considerably when compared to the zip code statistics in Figure 9.1 on page 143. We see the numbers nearly cut in half when just looking at the Troy School District, and the average sale price came down even more to just over $140,000. Affordability is the driving factor here, as 75% success rate is pretty good which could be due to the below-average sale prices.

When we combine the 12180 zip code with the Troy School District the numbers remain the same, for the most part. Apart from about 7 to 10 home sales, these numbers within the Troy School District represent our starting point for understanding where 9 Mason Street stands within the market.

We figured that a 90 day sale was possible, and we had a ball park sale price of $150,000, but we know it's not as cut and dry as this. Let's talk about the home style and the condition of the home to get a more accurate reading on the home's value and see how we made sure not to leave any money behind in the sale.

CONDITION

I talked about condition at length as one of the 5 Key Factors that lead to your asking price and a determining factor on how much you can sell your home for. The good news that I hope I conveyed is, you don't have to remodel, upgrade, or go crazy spending a lot of money to get your home ready to sell fast and for the most money.

9 Mason Street is a great example of this. This home could have surely used some upgrades. Maybe new carpet in the lower level, as well as hardwood flooring throughout the top floor. Or how about new kitchen countertops, cabinets and appliances? Don't forget about the furnace and water heater which will surely need attention in the next decade. Of course this could all be done, but it wasn't necessary, nor is it ever a necessity to remodel before you sell. To my client here at 9 Mason Street, this was going to be an "as-is" sale and I agreed.

I already touched on some features of this property before, but I'd like to add a few things here to give you a sense of the homes overall condition. What was great about this home was the fact that it had a 4th bedroom. With 3 bedrooms on the top floor, and a 4th bedroom created in part of the lower level, it had more than enough space for the next buyer to bring their family, or start one of their own.

It was a great family home, since my client raised five children in the home herself. And even apart from an oversized 4th bedroom in the lower level, it still had enough space that it boasted a big family room down there as well, complete with sliding glass door leading out to the back yard.

The next buyer for this home would plan to upgrade the heating and cooling system, as they were a bit outdated. The roof was about 17 years old but the shingles looked good, based on just an eye assessment, so we figured at least that the buyer would have peace on mind on not having to replace the roof anytime soon. Of course it was located in the city limits of Troy which means public utilities, so of course, no worries about a septic tank or private well.

The biggest draw for this home was the lot size. The entire neighborhood consisted of that suburban home feel where everyone at least, had a decent squared backyard, basically enough for a pool, and room for the pets and kids to enjoy.

9 Mason Street boasted one of the biggest lots in the entire neighborhood. With almost a half of an acre, the lot stretched far back to a point, and included privacy fence and some trees. As mentioned, the cul-de-sac setup of this home was an even bigger bonus. Lot size and layout matters a lot, and in this case, helped us greatly.

TAXES

Troy property owners are cringing with the recent tax hikes they had imposed in the 2016 calendar year. It has caused quite a stir and much controversy with what basically ended up being a 15% or so tax increase. 9 Mason Street, like other Troy property owners fell victim to this tax hike as well.

Despite my sellers Senior Citizen and STAR discounts, I marketed the home by publishing the actual taxes a new buyer will pay, without discounts. This way there are no surprises and home buyers can know exactly what their payment looks like.

For us, the total taxes on this home were just above $7,500 per year. This is a huge issue for the marketability of the home, and as we have learned, drives down overall sale price. It's no wonder the average sale prices in the 12180 and Troy School District are below the regions average.

In any event, we cannot do much about the taxes, except weigh them when we determine the asking price.

TIMING

Timing was perfect for us at 9 Mason Street. The market in 2016, leading into 2017 was performing well in our entire area, and I started the conversation with my seller in early May in regards to her plans on selling.

In just a few weeks, she was ready to go. I have to say, she was the type of selling client I wish I had more of. Understanding that the home needed to be clutter free was at the front of her mind, and she did a great job, with the help of family, getting the home to appear open and free of random items.

We listed the home at the end of May, which couldn't have been better. My seller understood the cyclical nature of our local real estate market, and with perennials and trees in bloom, there was no better time to market this great home.

As usual, I told my client that 90 days was the max amount of time I would like to spend on the market, but we both felt that this home had some unique qualities to it, and home buyers were surely to be interested.

THE SALE

We were live on May 22nd, 2017. Before I get to the results and our pricing schedule, let's see some additional proof on how we came about agreeing on the asking price for this home.

As we saw, the average sale prices in the Troy zip code and school district, hovered around $150,000. But what about Raised Ranch style homes, or better yet, what about the immediate neighborhood that proved to have no shortage of recent home sales for us to weigh?

Taking a quick look at some detailed 2016 statistics, we found 7 Raised Ranch home sales in the Troy School District, **and** within the

12180 zip code of course. Of those 7 home sales, we found that the average sale price was $172,045. About $30,000 higher than the overall averages in the Troy School District of $150,000.

What's more important was, these 7 sales were mostly 3 bedroom Raised Ranch homes, and we had a legal 4th bedroom at 9 Mason St. This was making us feel more confident.

Also, when looking at comparable sales just a street or two away, we found a few Raised Ranch home sales, one of which, was also a four bedroom home. It had been under contract for a few weeks, so we didn't know the sale price, but they were asking $199,000 and since it wasn't on the market long, we figured they must have accepted a deal in the $180's.

The difference with this immediate comparable sale was the fact that it was completely remodeled. Granite counter tops, hardwood flooring, an eccentric "man cave" with a bar and sports memorabilia, and also, a newer in ground swimming pool. I am not saying all these things will always make you more money, but as far as condition and perks went, this comparable home had it going on.

After all this research, and weighing the 5 Key Factors, we decided on going with an asking price of $184,500. A bit ambitions considering the high tax amounts and the somewhat outdated features of the home. But based on the current market, we went with this price, complete with professional photos that really made it stand out online.

Figure 9.3 on page 150, shows us our pricing schedule and final sale looked like for 9 Mason Street.

Figure 9.3: 9 Mason St. Home Sale Timeline

Date	Action	Price
5/22/2017	Listed for sale	$184,500
5/31/2017	Offer accepted	$175,000
7/18/2017	Closed sale price	$175,000

In just a matter of three days, we received an offer just $9,500 below asking price. This is a perfect example on how a home that was somewhat outdated, with high taxes, and located in a market with lower demand, was able to sell fast, and for a great price. We were able to use all the 5 Key Factors which lead to maximum profit and minimal stress for the home seller.

Notice how we stayed between the average sale prices for Raised Ranch style homes in Troy, and below a recent comparable sale, that was remodeled and asking $199,000.

We ended up selling for $3,000 over what Raised Ranch homes in Troy were averaging, and we received about 96% of our asking price. I love the 96% mark because that means our price was good enough for an offer, but also a bit too high. This is the best combination to get a home seller the best price. If we had listed the home lower, closer to $175,000, we could had possibly ended up with a full price offer, or even dropped down to the $170,000 mark.

Listing a great home, with a lot going for it, in prime home buying season, was also key. It's like casting a fishing line into a pool of hungry fish that haven't eaten in weeks. If we had listed the home in the Fall or

Winter, we would have been waiting a while to attract a home buyer during the slow season. A buyer who would have had time to focus on the negative aspect of high taxes and work needed, without feeling the threat of missing out to other home buyers.

9 Mason Street is a great case study due to the Troy real estate market being unforgiving. As the 20th ranked market in the region, and a recent tax hike, demand wasn't all that high. It's much harder to sell a home in a low demand area, as compared to that of Clifton Park or Saratoga. In fact, this Raised Ranch home would have gone for $250,000 in Clifton Park, with taxes closer to $5,000 per year. This is why the 5 Key Factors are so important to understand.

I thanked my seller client for being open minded to the current market conditions and having the wherewithal to get the home clutter free and show ready. It's important to put in the effort to make the home as presentable as possible, as it can add dollars to your final sale price.

This was a great example of a home that was a bit outdated, yet clean, that sold quickly for top dollar in a real estate market that had its history of struggling.

DEFEND YOUR EQUITY

CASE STUDY #5

By Ryan Hoffman

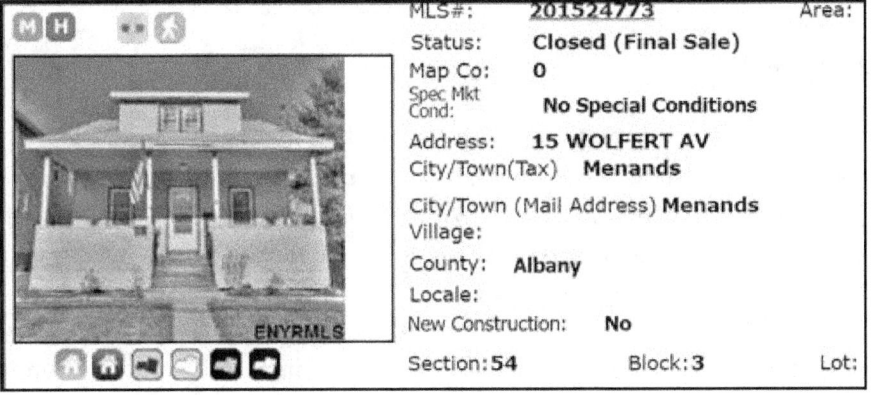

Address: 15 Wolfert Ave. Menands, NY

Zip Code: 12204

Zip Code Rank: 29th out of 70

School District: Menands (Choice)

School District Rank: 28th out of 49

THE DETAILS

15 Wolfert Avenue is a 90 year old, Craftsman Style home located in Menands, NY. It featured 3 bedrooms and 1.5 bathrooms and the size was around 1,200 square feet.

The lot itself was generous considering the age and the neighborhood, where other homes did not have quite as big of a yard size. The yard was fenced in and you could take a long driveway to the rear of the yard where there stood an oversized 2 car garage. The home was older, but had some upgrades and was very nicely decorated.

Let's breakdown the story of how this home lined up with the 5 Key Factors, and ultimately, how we got this home sold.

LOCATION

So you may be thinking, Menands? Maybe you have wondered what it would be like to live in Menands, but I assure you there are neighborhoods in Menands, away from the industrial overload, where good homes sit quietly in this small zip code.

In Menands, you're just a few minutes from entering the City of Albany. Heck if you work in downtown Albany, it would be a commute most would envy. You can also get to 787 quickly. And of course from there, in either direction, you have choices such as the Northway, or Interstate 90 making the location really ideal.

Another overlooked aspect to Menands is that although it is closer to the Hudson River, there are many streets that head west, up the hill into Loudonville, and even parts of Latham. Even a ride to Wolf Road is just 10 minutes away. Menands is a really tiny zip code geographically, and not all neighborhoods in the 12204 zip code are great places to buy. Menands can be easily overlooked by some home buyers, but definitely not all. In this case study, we see firsthand what a force this property turned out to be and how many buyers were paying attention.

So where does the 12204 zip code rank among all real estate markets, and what do the numbers look like? Let's check out the final data from 2016 in Figure 10.1.

Figure 10.1: 2016 Final Real Estate Sales for the 12204 Zip Code of Menands, NY

Homes Listed	Homes Sold	% Sold	Avg Price	DOM
73	47	64%	$247,827	56

Courtesy of the Eastern NY Regional Multiple Listing Service from 1/1/2016 to 12/31/2016

Wow. Now this is surprising to you maybe? We see an average sale price of $247,827? In Menands? That is almost $50,000 above the Capital Region average of $200,000.

Now, as an aside, let me quickly tell you that when I speak of a "Capital Region average sale price of $200,000", I am referring to the total home sales and final sale price averages of the four main counties combined. Menands is scoring a much higher average sale price, in only 47 sales. This small zip code didn't even list 100 homes in a year. Days on market were fast at just 56 days. All around, this market is looking pretty healthy. But how?

Being small geographically is something that cannot be helped. Zip codes such as 12065 (Clifton Park) and Troy (12180) just happen to cover more square miles. There are more homes to choose from, as well, and we see the evidence in the housing market statistics.

But what is great about the ranking system I had devised is, markets like Menands can still rank, and compete, against the bigger real estate markets. I have the Menands zip code of 12204 ranked 29th out of 70 zip codes I rank. Menands is able to rank higher, while being smaller, due to the fast sales and higher than average sale prices. It is also due to the fact that the Menands School District only reaches the 8th grade. Then parents have a choice of which high schools to send their children to, and some of those choices happen to be top school districts in our region.

SCHOOL DISTRICT

Menands High School? Never heard of it. Well, that's because it doesn't exist. I am sure you already knew that, but what you may not have known is the secret to success for Menands home sellers lies within this fact that no high school option exists.

For students graduating from the 8th grade in this district, parents then have a choice of what high school their kids can attend, and I can assure you parents love this. Especially because a couple of the choices happen to be two of the Top 5 School Districts in our rankings.

We talk about how important the school district is when it comes to selling your home and here, 12204 home owners, have the choice of five high schools their freshman kids could attend. Talk about having some serious selling power. These five schools include; Watervliet High School in the Watervliet School District, Colonie High School in the South Colonie School District, Shaker High School in the North Colonie School District, Heatly High School in the Green Island School District, and Tech Valley High School which is not located in a specific district.

If you have read this far, and I've explained things well enough, you may have just notice me mention those two schools that we know are in the Top 5 in our rankings. North and South Colonie School Districts.

Again, this creates serious leverage for a home owner looking to sell in the 12204 zip code. With multiple choices of schools, to which some are top ranked, home sellers have the upper hand in the sale and home buyers are happy to oblige, with average home sale prices close to $250,000.

The Menands School District real estate data is pretty scarce. Either way, let's take a look at Figure 10.2 for the final numbers in 2016 for the Menands School District to make a comparison to the zip code of 12204.

Figure 10.2: 2016 Final Real Estate Sales for the Menands School District.

Homes Listed	Homes Sold	% Sold	Avg Price	DOM
17	13	76%	$181,990	24

Courtesy of the Eastern NY Regional Multiple Listing Service from 1/1/2016 to 12/31/2016

One of the reasons for the low volume is due to the fact that local real estate agents are not marketing the home sales as being within the Menands School District. Instead, they list the homes with desirable districts attached to the listing as a way to entice home buyers. We see only 13 home sales. But still, 24 days on market average is still impressive. The numbers are good even though the sample size is really too small to make the best judgement.

Let's jump back to the 12204 zip code, and show you the 2016 home sale data, but this time, I have segmented them by school districts located in the 12204 zip code. See Figure 10.3 on the next page.

Figure 10.3: 2016 Final Real Estate Sales for the 12204 Zip Code, Segmented by School District

School	Homes Listed	Homes Sold	% Sold	Avg Price	DOM
Menands	17	13	76%	$181,900	24
North Colonie	38	24	63%	$338,940	61
Albany	18	10	56%	$114,745	85

We verify the Menands School District numbers are accurate, and now we see why average sale prices for the 12204 zip code are so high. 24 homes sold in the 12204 zip code that were actually designated to the North Colonie School District. We also see average sale prices at a whopping $338,940 for North Colonie district sellers. This is surely a boost to the overall averages in the zip code statistics. I know I sound like a broken record, but this is why segmentation matters.

For us at 15 Wolfert Ave, we care more about the Menands School District numbers. The good news is that since there is a choice of some good, high demand schools for parents to send their kids, it has certainly helped the average sale prices. While it won't compare to the North Colonie average prices of $330,000+, we definitely see Menands district home sellers getting a boost.

There are always reasons why differences exist in the data. This is why the style of the home, the age of the home, the square footage and all the other things we talked about in this book, are all huge factors into determining value. It may be a lot of work and research, but this is what needs to be considered and studied in order to have an ultimate pricing strategy. We are starting to see the perfect storm come to shape on this home sale. Let's move inside and talk about what this home had going for it.

CONDITION

This home was sleek and artfully decorated. Not bad for a 90 year old home. Hardwood floors throughout, newer vinyl windows, a roof that was less than ten years old, and of course, a remodeled kitchen. Nothing extravagant, but a great color scheme with the laminate countertops and stock cabinets.

Speaking of colors, the home was already painted very nicely, and the furniture was minimal, The home decor were perfect, and at the same time, it felt like a "home." Some problems existed, but what home pushing 100 years old doesn't have issues? The furnace and water heater were a bit dated, but still had no issues, and electrical checked out OK. The house was close to the street, but it had a good sized back yard, already fenced in and an oversized garage to go with it. These features alone are a big boost when it comes to home buyers wish list.

So here we have an affordable home that has character and perks. The condition is clutter free, clean, some upgraded features, plus the lot is great and a garage is a bonus. We have a good location in Menands and the choice of top schools. After this, not much else to cover when it came to this charming Craftsman style home.

Let's see how we lined up the last two Key Factors.

TAXES

The taxes were a slam dunk. $3,000 per year, give or take a few bucks, and yes, this is without STAR. Of course there are additional fees for water and sewer, but overall, the tax amounts on this home could not be better. Only South Colonie homes present such a low tax opportunity as this home did.

Not much else I can say about the taxes at this point. We know that the lower the overall taxes are on a property, the higher a home can sell for. In the case of 15 Wolfert Ave, we had low taxes going for us. We saw average sale prices over $180,000 when combing the 12204 zip code statistics with the Menands School District. These low taxes, and choices of great schools was the reason we flirted with an asking price of $180,000 for this home on Wolfert Ave.

TIMING

The timing for hitting the market was not ideal. We listed the home a week before Thanksgiving, not something I would advise. But, as talked about repeatedly, people have needs and sell for many different reasons.

For my clients here, they were in no rush. They were moving out of state and hadn't really made plans to transition to a life 600 miles away. They understood it could be a slow time of year, and not ideal for maximum price, but as we learned, many things trump timing. In our case, an affordable price, low taxes and top schools helped make up for our bad timing.

I explained all these factors leading up to the listing and told my clients to be prepared for a quick sale. However, they could stretch their time out even more by hiking their price up over what we agreed on. If you have time, who cares? While I am an advocate for a 90 day sale, and don't recommend sitting on the market too long, there are a few extenuating circumstances. Thanksgiving and Christmas being two of them. To limit ourselves to 90 days on the MLS wouldn't be logical since the holidays are wild card factors on timing. 120 to 150 days on market is a more realistic goal if you list it in November.

Don't forget that I don't agree with listing any home in the Fall or Winter. We saw where $5,000 or $10,000 can be left behind from sitting on the market during the slow times. But for us, we had an affordable price range, of under $200,000, which increased the buyer pool tremendously.

By no means were my clients worried about a fast sale, they may have just not expected their home to be so popular when it hit the market. The best part about Case Study #5 was, we did not use the Multiple Listing Service initially to market the home. Instead we used social media, specifically, Facebook, to create awareness and drive showings to the listing, then, in the end we used the MLS to make the deal happen.

THE SALE

This wasn't a typical sale that you may expect, or read about in Case Studies 1 through 4. This is because I utilized a different platform to gain exposure for a home that had a lot of leverage.

You may not know this about me, but I rely heavily on my own marketing and advertising to drive buyers to a home sale. Most home sellers sign a 6 or 12 month agreement to be placed on the MLS, then sit back to see what happens. This strategy is not a strategy at all, it's archaic.

In this new world of social connectivity and mobile technology, the real estate industry, while no stranger to threats, could be on the brink of collapsing under its own design.

Platforms such as Google, Facebook, and Zillow, all create opportunities to showcase anything on display, real estate especially, in an effort to gain attention and awareness. This is the game that we are really playing in real estate. Selling your home is simply about awareness. The more people that know your home is for sale, the better chance you'll have at selling it.

The old way to gain awareness and attention for your home, was to let a real estate agent submit it to the MLS, for a fee paid at closing, in exchange for exposure to all agents in the area and hope they are actually working with a buyer.

While this way still exists, and is capable of selling your home, there are other avenues for folks who wish to test the market a bit, without signing a contract, or want to avoid building a bad, online track record of your asking price. Like my folks here at Wolfert Ave who wished to list the home in November.

Since it was a bad time of the year to list a home, and since they were not in a hurry, I mentioned using Facebook as a way to gain awareness. It worked brilliantly. Showcasing and advertising the home through Facebooks powerful advertising platform, was single-handedly responsible for finding our home buyers.

As usual, professional photos were shot of the home, and with the flawless décor, the photos shined online. A one-page website was created that portrayed all of the photos and information, as well as contact information. We also announced an Open House in the Facebook ad, to see how big of a turnout we would receive.

Not only did the Facebook ad drive people to the website, they were made aware of our Open House and got access to the 50+ photos shot of the home. We started the ad on a Tuesday, with an Open House scheduled the coming Sunday.

As the week wore on, agents were calling me daily, wondering why the home wasn't on the MLS. This was a clear sign of interest, plus the hundreds of Facebook comments, shared posts, website visits, questions, calls and emails from interested buyers and their agents, was proof that this home had high demand.

We marketed the home for $169,000. This, of course, was part of the Facebook advertisement and displayed on the website. Sure enough the place was crawling with interested home buyers at the Open House and many bids followed in the days thereafter.

The results of this social media experiment cast a new angle that could be used to market and sell real estate. Without wanting to commit to the MLS and have their home stuck on the market without any control, this allowed us to present the home, and its price, anyway we wanted.

Facebook advertising allows the advertiser, in this case myself, to track and monitor the success of the ad. In conjunction with the website analytics, we can see how many visitors we have and how much engagement our advertisement builds. On Facebook, consumers chat amongst themselves in the comment section under the ad, so this provided us with instant feedback based purely on the photos and property information. This could all be used to pivot on our asking price, if needed.

Again, the game is awareness. Do we need other agents to tell their buyers about your home, and then sit and wait? Or can we just put your home in front of home buyers using powerful social media platforms and a few hundred dollars in ad spend?

We knew the Open House would be busy based on the response of the ad, and we were able to drive a sale without committing to an MLS agreement.

It's unlikely a real estate agent you choose would do this for you, let alone have the capacity to understand Facebooks in-depth advertising platform. They really just want to control the listing and they know once it hits the MLS, agents will bring buyers forward to see the home. And if things get quiet, the agents will just want you to drop the price. But that's the old, expensive route to selling your home, and it lacks strategy.

For the folks at 15 Wolfert, we were able to save them some money on the commission percentage since they expected to pay a real estate agent about 6% of the sale price. This is because without an MLS agreement, they were not obligated to pay any fees really. But once we got to working on a deal, with a buyer who already had an agent, we all agreed on a fair fee, and everybody went home happy.

Not much of a price schedule for you. "Listed" and Sold in a week. Again, out of default, since commission fees were paid, I had to post it in the MLS. It was fun to put a new listing in the MLS, except instead of "For Sale" we were "Under Contract" from day one.

Here is a look at Figure 10.4. The buyers for 15 Wolfert Ave worked out an agreement to let my clients stay in the house until past Christmas and the New Year (that is what you can do when you have real estate leverage). We closed in early March, but that was only due to this extended closing timeframe, plus bank holdups out of our control.

Figure 10.4: 15 Wolfert Ave. Home Sale Timeline

Date	Action	Price
11/20/2015	Listed for Sale	$169,000
11/20/2015	Offer accepted	$165,000
3/16/2016	Closing sale price	$165,000

We took a deal just $4,000 off the asking price, and this was from multiple bidders. We could have stayed firm but the buyers were able to pull on the sellers heart strings with a "Why I want to buy your home" letter, and if you think it's cheesy, boy does it work. In the end, not only was it a lesson on seeing the 5 Key Factors at play, it was also a big lesson about the what the future may hold when it comes to the way homes are marketed and sold.

Well, there you have it. 5 real life examples of sales made right here in our Capital Region, using the 5 Key Factors, and really, two dozen other factors that go into pricing and positioning a home to sell for the most money in the least amount of time.

15 Wolfert Ave proved to be my best case study to date. Between all of the 5 Key Factors acting strongly, plus the additional fact that the home was marketed through Facebook and not the Multiple Listing

Service, created an even more evolved strategy when it comes to selling homes.

I hope you enjoyed the journey on learning what it truly takes to sell your home. My wish is that the truth about the industry, and what drives your home to sell, can be found within the research and analysis of the local real estate market.

When you're ready to sell your home, be sure to work with an agent who possesses a documented approach and systematic pricing strategy like the one I laid out here. Or, if you'd like to try selling your own home, you can be rest assured that the tips, advice, and real life case studies in this book, can get you closer to handling the sale on your own when you price it properly.

Thanks again for taking the time to read this book. I hope you found it full of valuable information. And I hope you'll pass it along to a friend or family member who is looking for more insight into the real estate market themselves.

DEFEND YOUR EQUITY

HOW MUCH IS YOUR HOME WORTH?

You've read the book, now find out how much your home is *really* worth!

Forget Zillow and other online "instant" home valuation sites. You need a real pricing strategy behind the sale of your home to unlock its ultimate value.

Find out how much your home is worth in today's market with a FREE, online, in-depth video analysis of your home.

Let me take you inside the MLS with video analysis specifically created just for your home, and how it can be best positioned in the market.

You'll see:

- Real comparable home sales from your neighborhood as well as current real estate market conditions.

- Video Analysis of your home, complete with Google Street Views, Tax Record Reports, Sales History, and more!

- Your very own unique pricing strategy checklist so you can take advantage of all your homes unique features.

- And the opportunity for a home inspection, by a licensed NYS Home inspector with 40 years of experience. A $500 value, yours free.

Visit **www.DefendYourEquity.com** today and find out what your home is really worth in today's market, with a FREE video market analysis following the exact system laid out in this book.

DEFEND YOUR EQUITY

About the Author

Ryan Hoffman's clients are quick to call him "The Truth in Real Estate" due to his no-bull, straight forward approach to helping home sellers achieve their goal.

Ryan is often considered to be a Realtor by default due to his anti-gimmick, and anti-sales approach to selling real estate when working with clients. Using market research, and data analytics, Ryan helps home owners unlock their property's true potential by weighing it against the current market conditions, and the law of Supply and Demand.

With 8+ years' experience practicing real estate, Ryan has sold over $15 million dollars of real estate inventory single handily, right here in the Capital Region.

Ryan operates his business on the ideology of working closely with his select clients. His concern is not to employ dozens of agents and try to outsell the competition. Rather, Ryan focuses his work on home owners who are sitting on a large amount of equity that needs to be protected in the home sale.

Ryan fights to get the highest price possible for his clients homes, in an industry that typically operates on fast turnover, Ryan believes in providing around-the-clock care to all his clients to be sure things run smoothly all the way to the closing table.

Ryan developed and manages, the first and only, real estate ranking index of its kind in the Capital Region. Using real estate market statistics and a simple computer algorithm, Ryan keeps a close watch on the Capital Region real estate market by tracking and ranking 70 zip codes and 39 school districts, to measure their performance and see wherein lies the highest demand that home owners can take advantage of.

He also uses in-depth research to get to the core of what makes a home sell for the most money.

Ryan is a full time New York State Licensed Real Estate Broker and operates his business from his home office that he shares with his wife Erin, and two, four-legged "kids", Teddy and Charlie.

Ryan owns and operates Leverage Real Estate LLC, where he keeps folks up to date on the current real estate market conditions, and shares more inside tips and techniques to both buying and selling a home.

Check out **www.RyanJHoffman.com** to follow along with Ryan and to learn more about how you can accomplish your real estate goals.

www.ingramcontent.com/pod-product-compliance
Lightning Source LLC
Chambersburg PA
CBHW071208240526
45470CB00018B/1588